If He Ain't Mr. Right, He's Mr. Wrong

Written, compiled and edited

By

Pamelia Tyree-Carr

1

If He Ain't Mr. Right, He's Mr. Wrong
Printed in the United States of America

ISBN 978-0-9843245-9-0

Published by: Parablist Ministries Inc.
P.O. Box 43379
Richmond Heights, OH 44143

If He Ain't Mr. Right, He's Mr. Wrong

Contributors

Michael Clifton
Jacqueline Gillon
Sikandar Z. Hameen
Lucky Caswell Harris
Princess Harris
Florine Jones
Claudene McCoy
Tierra Morman
Havana Newbridge
Desmond Pringle
Lisa Rodriquez
December Rose
Walter Simpkins
Tuesday Tate
Aaron B. Thomas
Alan Washington
Kim Whitmore
Shermelle Wilson
Deborah A. Wright

Forward
Deborah A. Wright

Cover Design and Layout
Deborah A. Wright

Photo of Author
Akemi Carter

Disclaimer

This book is not intended to replace the advice of a professional counselor. The purpose of this book is to share life experiences of the author and other women, who have contributed their stories to provide awareness as well as encouragement to women and men seeking healthy relationships.

The various topics of this book are concise and to the point. This book may not contain perfect American English or grammar. In addition, the language often borders on colloquialism to reflect current dialogue of today. In the interest of privacy, some names have been changed.

This book contains adult content and is not intended for persons under the age of 18.

*T*able of Contents

Dedication

In memory of my father, Gilbert Pittman who taught me to follow my heart, trust my own feelings and to live life to the best of my ability. My father was also the first man who gave me a real talk about sex, lies and infidelity as well as important information regarding how to discern "Mr. Wrong" from "Mr. Right".

In loving memory of my aunt Grace Bennett who loved me unconditionally who passed on September 12, 2010.

In loving memory of Yasuko Carter-Boyer the author of *How Cancer Saved My Life: I Won't Shed Another Tear,* who took the time to write a letter of encouragement, in the midst of all she was going through with cancer. God allowed me to come across that letter, long after she had departed this world and find encouragement in a devastating time in my life. The vision that she shared in that letter resulted in this book being written. Rest in peace Yasuko, you are not forgotten.

"Men are always where they want to be, so don't go searching for them. You might find something you really don't want to know."

Gilbert Pittman

8

Acknowledgments

To my heavenly Father who keeps on making a way for me. To God be the glory for the things that he has done. Because of His redeeming love, I can live life from this day forward with no regrets.

To my children, LaJoy, Milton and Michael who have the job assignment of watching me through my growing pains. They help protect me from this cold, cold world regardless of the situation, when I have fallen and even when I am standing tall. To my granddaughter, De'Ja who believes in my dreams and often tells me not to give up because big dreams will happen. To my grandson Da'Vonn who keeps me on my toes and who I truly believe one day will know who I really am, since he now calls me by three different names.

To Quincy W. Carr, Jr. who continues to encourage me to move away from any dry brooks and to continue to move forward towards the destiny that God has called me to. He often reminds me of the scripture found in Jeremiah 29:11 "For I know the thoughts that I think towards you, saith the Lord, thoughts of peace, and not of evil, to give you an expected end."

To Jesse O. Nixon, Sr., my grandfather who taught me, "When you get to the end of your rope, tie another knot and hold on!"

To my Aunt LaClair who raised me since the age of eight. Thank you for giving me the best advice ever: "Hold on to at least one piece of yourself, for one day the right man will come along. If you don't hold on to something, you won't have anything to offer him."

9

To Mr. Kim Richardson who is always right on time with his words of encouragement. Kim constantly reminds me to remain focused and to keep in mind that I am the head and not the tail.

To Brenda Kirby, words cannot express how much I love you. Every time I say your name, a smile comes across my face. Because of you, I had to have my assigned seat changed in Church.

To Gilbert Glenn King, who is my friend for life who I have known since the age of twelve and has taught me to live, love, and laugh.

To Nadjra Washington, who because of her voice of wisdom and encouragement has helped me during several trying times during the course of my life.

To Deborah A. Wright, for her tireless long hours spent formatting and reading this book over and over to make sure it flowed in the right direction. Deborah also kept me on point, with words of encouragement when I felt like giving in and giving out. She constantly reminded me of the importance of completing this project, that she felt would benefit countless women and men, for "such a time as this."

To Havana Newbridge for going the extra mile using her gift of editing. Havana helped to make sure this project arrive to the publisher in a timely fashion.

To Bonnie Copes, Velma Jordan, Claudene McCoy and Evelyn Nixon who helped me get to the finish line with this book project, by taking time from their busy schedules to help with proofing.

To Linda Miller-Davis who has always taken time to encourage me and speak positive words into my life.

To Vickie Bearden, who knows most of my secrets. Thanks for keeping my hair done in excellence. It's amazing the information you can get out of a person while shampooing their hair.

To Shermelle Wilson for her marketing skills and assistance in helping to make the first video trailer of the book.

To Michael Clifton, Sikandar Z. Hameen, Desmond Pringle, Walter Simpkins, Aaron Thomas, and Alan Washington for giving their words of wisdom concerning finding healthy relationships and how to arrange our lives to reflect our major priorities.

A special thanks to every women who contributed to this book, by taking off their masks, in an effort to give women as well as men a different perspective on making better choices when choosing their mates. Although most of their struggles represent warnings from their various life experiences, they were all careful not to leave the taste in our mouths that as the saying goes, "All men are dogs."

To my cousin Denise Harrington and her daughter Brittany who started planning my book signing for the Atlanta area prior to the book actually being delivered. That is what I call truly believing in me. Not just for this book going forth, but also in my other major projects.

To David L. McAllister who I appreciate more than words can say for continuously believing in me.

This book is dedicated to the eleven women who lost their lives on Imperial Avenue in Cleveland, Ohio; as well as in loving memory of Tonya Lanice Hunter-Lyons (February 17, 1968 - July 25, 2010), who was a licensed independent marriage and family therapist and chemical dependency counselor who lost her life due to domestic violence.

Forward

*B*race yourself! Pamelia Tyree-Carr has written this book with her signature "straight talking, pull the cover off of the butt naked truth approach", no holds barred. She often says, "God can't heal what you won't reveal."

Like Harriet Tubman, Pamelia is fearless when it comes to "returning back" if it means being able to lead "a fellow diva" out of bondage and into the boundless freedom that awaits them through Christ.

Pamelia takes a strong approach, when it comes to helping women heal from the battle wounds inflicted on so many, by the unrelenting pursuit of finding a "good man". Pamelia's message is raw. She does not soften or sugar coat it. She tells it like it is. She feels that the problem with most Christians today, is that they act as though they have been saved, sanctified and speaking in tongues all of their lives. They simply fast forward, skip by and delete certain chapters in their story, not realizing that their mess just may be the "message" someone else needs to get their act together.

Pamelia believes that others are lost and hurting (especially in the Church) because we choose to sit with our double-lace hankies over our $40.00 stockings and fail to remember the times we were out there, "looking for love in all the wrong places." If the truth be told, many, while actively serving in our local Churches, or as Pamelia says in one of her plays and as evidenced by the stories in this book, many God-fearing, Bible toting, preaching, teaching women of God are "going to hell with gasoline drawers on!"

No longer can we take the passage in Titus Chapter Two and relegate it to cleaning toilets and baking biscuits. The world is "teaching" hard and we have got to "preach" it hard! Pamelia's message is for the Rahabs, Gomers, Tamars, Leahs, Esthers, Potiphar's Wives, Hagars and Mother Jenkins of today!

If He Ain't Mr. Right, He's Mr. Wrong, was written to simply "help a Sistah out". This book has several stories from contributors who were more than willing to aid Pamelia's heart-felt cause. This book is much more than a set of "juicy" stories, but designed to "give God the glory" as it enables serious Sistahs to reveal the devil's plot, stay off his turf and to finally stop the madness in their lives!

The Bible is so true about being "unequally yoked". A lot of "Baby Daddy Drama", can be avoided by knowing the telltale signs of the many "Mr. Wrongs" they likely encounter each day. Mr. Wrong preys on women who do not know their true worth in Christ and/or seek to be accepted at any cost or just simply blinded by the romanticism of having a man, any man. This book also shows you how to recognize, "Mr. Right", who all too often has been waiting on the sidelines all along. It is dedicated to the "Mr. Rights" of the world who have just simply gotten a raw deal. Keep doing what you do. It is definitely a new day, and we are waking up and smelling the coffee! Or, in the words of one of Pamelia's friends…"So long Mr. Wrong!"

Deborah A. Wright

Introduction

*In that day seven women will take hold of one man and say,
"We will eat our own food and provide our own clothes;
only let us be called by your name. Take away our
disgrace!"*

Isaiah 4:1 (New International Version)

During the course of a lifetime, we tend to meet
some people who look good on the outside, but are ugly on
the inside - they are what I call a dressed up mess! We
have a notion that these individuals are not right, not just
for us personally, but, not even for our close friend. This is
when I suggest you follow your first mind or as the saying
goes, "Run for the border!"

In my opinion, we as women should take inventory
of who we are allowing to occupy our space. We should
also know what we are looking for in a man and require a
self-check in the very beginning. Some women see clearly
that they are about to step into the twilight zone long before
the friendship starts.

Within the first few days, we have the ability to see
when and where the mess has started, and to know exactly
when we will need to put our boots on, in order to walk in
the mess, just in case the situation gets too deep.

Just as there are three levels to knowing God: the
outer court, the inner court and behind the veil; in most
cases, the men we allow to enter the outskirts of our lives,
are not worthy to take the next step into the inner courts of
our thought processes. In some instances, they will almost
never deserve to know us within the secret area where our
soul resides, which is behind the veil.

15

At the wedding, most brides wear a veil. Once the veil is lifted by her husband, it indicates that he is the only one worthy of getting to know everything about his bride. At that point, he has already passed the test and is qualified to be her covering.

Before selecting a man, which is more than likely a temporary solution to a permanent problem, stop to find out if he's worthy of your time, your money, your love and/or your affection.

I often get really upset with myself, when I look back over my life, and think of how many situations I allowed to happen to me. Situations where I did not always take the time to get to know the individuals that I allowed inside my head and into my heart too fast. They were not worthy and had not proven themselves to me. I had first given them my mind, then afterwards, my body and soul followed. I have learned what the true meaning of a soul tie really is and how hard it can be to break the yoke, which had wrapped, tied, and tangled my soul until I met the man who can destroy the yokes. His name is Jesus.

I can remember when I first realized I had a lot of issues. The following analogy will describe how it all began:

I stopped by the store to purchase a pouch to carry my items in. Then I purchased an arm bag, a small piece of luggage, luggage with a long strap, luggage on wheels, one piece of designer luggage, and finally a trunk with a designer logo. By the time I realized I really had a lot of hurt to carry, I purchased a car to put my entire luggage in, to hide what was really going on. I intentionally misplaced the key, so I would not have the ability to unlock the trunk.

When I arrived at my final destination, after living with several individuals and walking as if I was the "walking dead" through three marriages, I decided it was time to unpack. I had lots of junk in my trunk. So, I had a key made in order to open up the trunk so I could prepare to unpack my hurt on people in the relationships that I was in. These were people who truly did not understand what was really going on; which was simply that, I had been hurt over and over and over again. As you already know, hurt people, hurt people.

If you are anything like me, you want to be loved 365 days a year. One of my favorite lines from one of the plays I wrote says, "I'd rather have nothing, than to have something and still have nothing." Most women pray, "Lord, please send me the right man", while they have one on hold, in layaway and/or have a man that they hand picked themselves. My Bible tells me that "He, who finds a wife, finds a good thing." The key word here is "He" not "She". My father used to say, "Pam, no man wants a woman who is hiding in the bushes with her safari suit on yelling, here I am, I'm over here." "Why do you look for the living among the dead?" Luke 24:5(b) NIV. You want to know that you have someone in your life who has your back whether you are rich or poor, in good times and bad times, and last but not least, for better or for worse.

We, as women, must stop taking care of men who do not care for us. We must learn sound values to live by when selecting a mate, from the one-night stands, all the way to the altar. The old folks used to say, "Why buy the cow, when the milk is free?" My grandmother used to say "Pamelia, if you don't stand for something, you will fall for anything." On several occasions, I let my body make what I felt was a sound decision, for that moment anyway. When I did not want Mr. Right nor Mr. Wrong, just Mr.

17

Right Now, I woke up in places, (mentally as well as physically), where I thought I would never be. I had a counter ego who I named Faye, (Faye is my middle name), as I faded into the background of my own life. This was my way of dealing with what, eventually, became major depression and sometimes, thoughts of suicide, when I just could not handle the person I had become.

I would have the nerve to bring various individuals to my family gatherings that I, personally approved of, but knew right away, that my family would not. (Especially, since I am from a very religious family, who will chew you up, keep the meat, and throw out the bones.) My family is my family. You can choose your friends, but not your family.

I would enter into the room with an individual smiling from cheek to cheek, with an outfit on that they more than likely, would not approve of either. When my grandmother would be seated in her favorite chair, at the head of the dining room table, I would hear her say "Just look what the cat has dragged in now." That simply meant, he was not the one. If you take into consideration what older women have to say, in most cases, they really do have the answers you have been looking for. That is why I feel every woman needs someone to give her sound instructions like the example in Titus Chapter Two. "Then they can train the younger women to love their husbands and children to be self-controlled and pure." Titus 2:4-5a (NIV)

Hopefully, you will enjoy the next few chapters of *"If He Ain't Mr. Right, He's Mr. Wrong"*, which I have taken time to make sure you have a clear understanding of what sex, lies, and infidelity really look like. I have used some of my personal experiences, notes from my diary, letters I wrote to various individuals, and last but not least, a Soul Ties prayer and letters from women, who I know personally. In most cases, names have been changed to protect the innocent. Once you have completed reading this book, I pray that you will have restoration for your mind, body, and soul. In addition, I am in hopes that you will come out as the victor and no longer the victim.

Be Liberated,

Pamelia Tyree-Carr

Amazing Grace Lyrics

John Newton (1725-1807)
Stanza 6 anon.

Amazing Grace, how sweet the sound,
That saved a wretch like me.
I once was lost but now am found,
Was blind, but now I see.

T"was Grace that taught my heart to fear.
And Grace, my fears relieved.
How precious did that Grace appear
The hour I first believed.

Through many dangers, toils and snares
I have already come;
"Tis Grace that brought me safe thus far
and Grace will lead me home.

The Lord has promised good to me.
His word my hope secures.
He will my shield and portion be,
As long as life endures.

Yea, when this flesh and heart shall fail,
And mortal life shall cease,
I shall possess within the veil,
A life of joy and peace.

When we've been here ten thousand years
Bright shining as the sun.

We've no less days to sing God's praise
Than when we've first begun.

Amazing Grace, how sweet the sound,
That saved a wretch like me.

I once was lost but now am found,
Was blind, but now I see.

Chapter 1

The Letters

Will:

This is a brief note to say thank you for helping to lighten the "loneliness" I've experienced for the past several months, (although several people were around me). I am in hopes that this will be the beginning of a fruitful friendship. It is important to me that I don't feel as though I'm going through life all alone.

Several people have passed though my life within the last 37 years and I've seen a lot of good and bad times. Therefore, I am starting to be extremely careful as to who I give my feelings to. I'm sure you can understand where I'm coming from.

Although I've lived the past three (3) years in a relationship with someone that I felt obligated to, (indirectly anyway, especially, since he's a married man who takes care of most of my physical and financial needs), I've still spent several hours tied up in various projects to help the time go by faster. I'm not really into the waiting game, but, I've put myself into this position so I deal with it. Since I met you, I feel as though I have something to look forward to even though it may be in the wee hours of the night. When I hear your voice over the telephone (although I've been half-asleep), it makes me feel warm on the inside. By the time you arrive, I am moist (Smile). It's at the point now that I'm anticipating whatever might take place between us; although, I refuse to feel as though I'm getting your leftovers. I'm sure you mentioned when we talked that you are a single man. You are single aren't you?

I do plan on keeping a diary of this relationship or should I call it a friendship? Let's just go with the flow. What will be, will be.

The chocolate candy, which you will receive along with this letter, is just to remind you of how sweet I am, (Ms. Candy Kisses - smile). I guess I'll keep you around a little while longer, since you make me feel good all over. Even though we've just met, I feel you are my soul mate and I've known you for a long while. From our long conversations, we seem to really understand each other.

All I'm really trying to say is thanks for putting a smile on my face, and having the knowledge of knowing how to keep it there.

Hope that we can be together soon,
Pamelia

May 27, 1997
(47 days later...)

Will:
This is a brief line or two to bring you up-to-date on where my feelings are at this point of the game. I gave writing you this letter a lot of thought. I decided that you more than likely cared enough to at least read this note. It contains most of my feelings, that you really don't have time to listen to, during your rush hours.

When I met you in March, I thought we could get together every now and then, and eat lunch and/or dinner in your spare time. However, after being around you so frequently, I saw other potential in our relationship. I started to feel as though the feelings had to be mutual, but at this point, I feel like I'm out on the field, alone again.

It seems to irritate you when I make such comments as, "I need to talk to you, to see where your head is." "Why haven't I seen you more than once since you've returned home?" You suddenly have to hang up and it's almost as though you are running from something. What are you running from, may I ask? I really do not have time for games and I felt as though you were a safe person to give my heart to, but lately, you seem to have made a decision about our friendship, but somehow, decided to leave me out of the decision making process.

Today, when I asked were you coming by this evening or not, you made another shocking comment of "I'm trying to get my life back together." I was there for you when you said your life was falling all apart, (when you had unexpected visitors according to you in your home). My making the decision to allow you to stay at my house caused a lot of changes in my normal lifestyle. I was more than happy to try and make you comfortable by any means necessary. I am in hopes that you will at least put yourself in my shoes, if only for one moment and try to see how left out I am feeling.

I mentioned to you when I first met you that I wanted a hassle free relationship and I still feel the same. If you don't have time for me while you "get your life back in order", I will step to the side and allow you the room you need to grow. But there is one catch to it, and that is, you take time to explain to me if I should continue to wait on you. At this point, I don't know if I should continue to be angry or if it even matters to you. I am too old to play guessing games. I'm willing to leave all the emotional part of this friendship out and simply be as we began . . . as friends.

Even though it is impossible to try and look inside of your heart. I, sometimes, think I know you a little bit. I experienced a major void suddenly, when you dropped the bomb on me that you really did have a woman in your life on a serious basis. I feel as though I had to be rushed to the emergency room following that drastic conversation. (I'm sure you recall the tears and illness behind all that drama). But since that time, I've taken a reality check as far as we are concerned. When I'm alone (waiting to hear from you), I can hear you say, "Pam, I never committed myself to you." I'd hate to see what commitment really means to you.

Let's at least take time to talk so I'll know what direction I'm going. I really need to know where your feelings lay. I'm a big girl; I can take it whichever way you choose. The ball is in your court, or is the game over? It's not that I'll stop eating. It's more like I'll keep my feelings to myself, just to be safe.

Can't get you off my mind,
Pamelia

May 29, 1997
(2 days later)

Will:

I thought of you today and decided to write a poem, which I am dedicating to you, called, "Chasing Ghosts". This poem came to me as I sat waiting to hear from you, but, for some reason the phone never rang! One of the questions I asked myself was, "Do I ever cross your mind?" The poem goes a little something like this:

27

Chasing Ghosts

Chasing ghosts too blind to see
Chasing ghosts wondering
if there will ever be
a you and a me
Chasing ghosts wondering when,
you'll ever be a part of my world again.
Had a strange experience today.
I found the ghost
and here's what he had to say,
The past is the past,
the present is the present,
look to the future
for which you can clearly see
For there never was a you and a me.

Signed,
The wait is over!

"There's a thin line between loneliness and desperation."
Pamelia Tyree-Carr

Chapter 2

The Different Types of Men

Like Father –Like Son

*F*rom the very moment a boy child is born, he becomes attached to his first teacher…his father. His eyes study his father constantly. During the initial bonding process, he learns to smile and form other mutual communication techniques. He, as with any other cub, is taught survival skills; how to eat, dress, bathe, use the toilet, general manners and obedience—most implied by a look, or spoken in a certain tone of voice. He is able to understand the language long before he can speak it.

Throughout his lifetime, he never stops studying and learning from his father. He learns glances, body language and moods, including but not limited to the spoken and unspoken messages that his father displays. As the cub, he mimics and includes these practices, right or wrong, as part of his survival skills from the very start.

By the time the boy reaches his teens, he is fully schooled in the various manipulative skills available to be used on women. These opinions have been formed from various avenues that he has encountered in his life, such as television, Hollywood movies (i.e., "The Mack"), true romance magazines, and love songs, as well as, rap music and last but not least, his peers. He is made to believe that these are documents of truth that he must adhere to in order to be accepted into the "manhood club". Therefore, the teen years are spent trying out various schemes on females to test their reactions, sincerity, and level of interest. He is well-versed by this time, to sift through whatever the female says, and is able to decide what she really means and what her reaction should be.

As the years go by, the man grows and develops his skills of survival and level of intelligence and eventually lands in a place that his practices lead him to. There are several levels of manhood that he can strive for. Each level of lifestyle choice is predicated solely by his dreams, ambition and goals. The higher the goals, the more sophisticated he will be.

The woman must be aware of the various types of men that are available to her. Her selection process must be based upon her own individual needs and wants. It is imperative to recognize that while trying to change some things about ourselves, we must also develop an intolerance of certain behaviors from others. A major part of self-care is being unwilling to accept another person's abuse and/or violence of any kind towards you. Whether it is mental, physical, verbal or financial abuse.

Caring for yourself psychologically and emotionally includes but is not limited to:

Paying attention to the tapes in your head. Who is talking? What are they saying? Do you need to begin erasing and/or changing these tapes to make them more positive?

Warning Signs

Most women see the warning sign but refuse to read them. Ones like:

No U Turn, Under Construction

Use Caution, Hidden Drive

Hot Surface Do Not Touch

Keep Out

No Trespassing

Open Hole

Open Pit

Restricted Area

Do Not Enter Authorized Personnel Only

Danger-Watch Your Hands, Fingers, Eyes and Ears

Protection Required In This Area

Go Slow

Open Door Slowly

Not An Entrance

Not An Exit

Watch Your Head

Watch Your Step

One Way Only

Forbidden Fruit

There are several forbidden fruit when it comes to dealing with men. Some women choose to steer clear of forbidden fruit while others want to take the Adam and Eve route. (You can eat this, but do not eat that). We have all been there, that fine, physically and financially fit man, who due to obvious circumstances, is better left alone. But, some can resist everything but temptation. Temptation is only a test of our character. In most cases, women soon find out that the odds are stacked against us.

While we are on the subject of relationships, let us not forget the mistake we make when we enter into a new relationship, we become too intimate too soon. We seek romance without finance. I wish I had a dollar for every time I have come across a woman who thought her new relationship was progressing when seemingly out of nowhere it fell apart. We end up left all alone with one question, why didn't he just say something?

What God has for me is for me. There are plenty of Mr. Rights out there, we just need to prepare ourselves emotionally, spiritually and financially. If you want an unhappy life - and this is a guarantee - get involved with a man merely for the sake of having one. Most of the men I just described are simply for flesh reasons only, also known as Mr. Feel Good. The emptiness most of us feel, can only be fulfilled by God only. There is a thin line between alone and lonely.

"God will always give us a way to escape. The problem is we don't always take it."

Pamelia Tyree-Carr

The Big Penis, Little Penis Syndrome

The first type man is very aware of the size of his penis and bases his entire life on how many women and men as well, are aware that he is "holding". The rude awakening is soon to come. However, when he wakes up and sees that the average woman is looking for love in all the wrong places and has lowered her standards to meet her physical needs, then his ego is deflated. He spends 90% of his life pleasing himself by sleeping with 2-3 women per day to show his stability. The rude awakening comes when he finds out he is not "an Eveready® battery" and will not take a licking and keep on ticking. The big penis man carries himself in a very sure way, whereas he feels that all women are looking for "good love" (as Anita Baker says) and that he is the answer to their prayers.

This type of man normally has not held a good paying job or more than likely never has been employed. Especially since, the women in his life have allowed themselves to become caught up in this madness and have taken care of his every whim and cry for this and cry for that, especially his financial needs. Little does she know, that she is one in a million and that he has it in his mind that he is God's gift to ALL women, not just her alone. In addition, he has several other women whom he may or may not make publically known. He feels he cannot be replaced and that he has it "going on" to the point that you cannot do without him.

The big penis man has the greater advantage of having women cater to him and making provisions for him. He has been known to own several cars, houses, and land while lying on his back being fed grapes from his woman's hand. His lovemaking has been compared to "Mississippi Mud Pie", better than sex itself.

36

On the other hand, the little penis man has been known to hold as many as two to three jobs at once and cannot find a woman worthy of his labor. He leads a very lonely life and usually has fine cars and a very nice home, which he has worked day and night to obtain. He is prepared to be a good father to the children he may or may not have had and in addition, he is willing to take care of an "instant" family if necessary.

A sure way to find this type of man is to take notice of the man who is leaning on the wall while out partying and who has very little or anything to say to the women who walk by. This man, as quiet as it is kept, is constantly overlooked by the average woman. However, he is the answer and the method to her madness. As the old saying goes, "it's not the size of the ship, but the motion of the ocean." However, he still has the sexual skills to make up for his shortcomings. Therefore, it is not necessary to try to find out the size of a man's penis by the size of his shoes and/or the size of his hands, and last but not least, by his weight nor height. Some good things do actually come in small packages.

It is imperative that we as women no longer choose a man according to his bed abilities, but instead his ability to love and cherish us. In return, we will have no other choice but to honor and respect him regardless of his sexual abilities.

Lack of Personal Hygiene

The main question is, "Did you at least drink some water today?" This type man believes firmly in the deodorant commercial which says, "Five days later and I'm still fresh." It is impossible to remain fresh all day long after shooting basketball with the fellas, working all day, and then expect to make love all night long. In my opinion, he should present his body as a living sacrifice! Because of his beliefs, he is cheated out of the best things in life; especially since his lovemaking will surely become limited. In addition, women are turned off the moment he walks by.

In some cases, you may be in the process of romancing him by running a hot tub of water and decide to run to the store. On your way out, you let him know that the water is for him and that his clean underwear etc. is lying next to the tub. When you return, he is still sitting in the same location with his feet up watching TV and flicking the remote. This is extremely aggravating. He also has been known to spray on loud cologne, over an unwashed body. Motto to live by: "Thou shall not request special sexual favors without taking the first step…water!"

Am I Gay or Straight? The Boy Toy

This is a very sensitive topic; however, it was impossible to leave it out of a book of this nature.

One hot summer day, I stepped up on the city bus and saw a close friend of mine, whom I attended Junior and Senior High School with. In addition, I thought I knew this individual well. "Hello Ralph", I said, as I started towards him. With anger he replied, "My name is no longer Ralph, I would appreciate it if you would call me Regina, Ms. Thing!" Several weeks went by and I saw "Regina" at a local bar along with a few of his...or maybe I should say her friends.

A nice looking man started walking towards us and extended his hand for a dance, I started to get up out of my seat and low and behold, he was not asking me for the dance, but Regina instead! This is when my eyes became completely opened and I found out that I simply did not have the right combination for his lock. This was a total shock, especially, since the songwriter said, "I need a good woman bad." As they began to dance on the slow song, winding and grinding each other as if they were already in bed, he began to whisper sweet nothings in Regina's ear. The audience sat, patiently, watching this masquerade.

The song finally ended, but before they sat down, the man reached over and kissed Regina on her lips. This amazed the people who were watching and waiting to see how this foolishness would finally end. He escorted Regina to her seat and told the Bar Maid to send her whatever she was drinking as they exchanged phone numbers.

Later that night, when I saw Regina in the Ladies Room (of all places), she was complaining about the button which popped off of her skirt while the man she was dancing with rubbed "all over my behind", as she stated. This may sound unreal, but listen up...

One evening my girlfriend and I decided to eat at a nice local restaurant in our city. When the waiter approached us, he mentioned that he knew a few of the people my girlfriend worked with. (He recognized the uniform she was wearing). "Mr. Waiter", started to call off names of men who my girlfriend might know from her station. He rattled on and on and finally, mentioned a name she recognized. "Mr. Waiter" repeated the name and mentioned the name of the man's wife. We began to question him about this man, especially since we knew him well. We were eager to get all the gossip and hot information. We let "Mr. Waiter" know that we were very familiar with this man, but we did not know his wife. "Well", he began, "the reason why his wife and I don't get along is because I...well you know..." We both started to stare at each other and replied, "Well you know what?" in one voice. "Well, I was his lover and she found out." We held our mouths opened wide and said, "Impossible!" "This is a real man and every woman at the station says so", we replied.

"Mr. Waiter" continued on to say, "Have you ever been to bed with him?" "Girlfriend, I can prove it. I have made love to him several times. Did the women he made love to tell you that he has a mole on the tip of his penis? That's the part about him I hate the most, that mole!" At this point, we were on the floor of the restaurant laughing.

40

However, all jokes aside, this is not a laughing matter. The Bible is true, "What is done in the dark will soon come to the light."

"Girlfriend", (as he rolled his eyes towards the ceiling), he continued, "You have more than likely lost men to me too!"

A few of the reasons he gave us were as follows:

- Lack of attention towards our man;

- Not attending to his every need.

Simple things like:

- running his bath water and placing wine on the side of the tub;

- making love by candle light;

- picking the hairs from his chin;

- fixing his favorite meal;

- giving him compliments on the way he looks;

- rubbing his stinky feet after a hard day's work;

- giving him back rubs;

- and making love to him more than once a month.

"Mr. Waiter" also said that when a man needs a shoulder to cry on, our man knows where to find him, because he is sitting by the phone, instead of running the streets.

His motto: "When you won't, I will!" One other important piece of advice he gave, "I always keep one good looking woman as my friend. Simply because where there is honey, the bees will follow." In other words, the men will come chasing after the woman and "Mr. Waiter" will benefit from the catch, if the man is open minded enough. My girlfriend and I made a vow to never be guilty of any of the things listed above...ever!

The gay man that is in limbo can be found at parties observing the women he is seeking to devour. He has not made it known to the public that he is straddling the fence. Because the woman is usually laughing and listening to corny jokes, and has had one drink too many; she is not prepared for the sting. He walks over to her with a very deep voice, looking good and smelling good and tells her, "Baby, I've been watching you all night, may I have this dance?" She is so flattered by the attention she is receiving, that she sits down and begins to hold a long drawn out conversation with him after the dance. He gets her number and offers to take her home even though she came out with her girlfriend. She tells her girlfriend good-bye as she gets into his new Lexus.

When they arrive at her apartment, he continues to talk with her and lingers over an hour. By this point, she is so interested in what he has to say, she allows him to come up for a nightcap. The nightcaps ends up being her instead of what was originally intended.

During the process of making love to him, she notices a difference in his techniques. His penis will not get up regardless of how sexy she may look. The emotion lotions and body oils do not work. Not even magic or

Louisiana root would help at this point. It might even be necessary to call 911 for help.

Questions begin to run through her mind as she lays there looking at the ceiling while he pretends to fall asleep. This has answered his questions. The answer being that women just do not turn him on anymore.

The man who does not miss a beat is called Brother Lovelady; he loves both the women and the men and plays his hand undercover. One of his favorite pastimes is looking at men's boodies, instead of Judy's. He can be found in local gay bars late at night, searching and hoping to be plucked from the group. He has at least two girlfriends during the day. He desires to be "had" by a man, if only for one night. The women who are involved in this madness think highly of this individual and know absolutely nothing about his wandering through time as he goes searching for the same thing she is looking for...a good man with good love.

This type of man also beats his women for no apparent reason, because he is extremely aggravated with his lifestyle of having to go undercover, to get his pleasures. He often tells the men he meets that he has a woman, a good job and is faithful to his home Church. Therefore, the man who he deals with will not be allowed to put him out in the open, simply, because he has a lot to lose. He has sex with both men and the women and still finds himself searching for the ultimate. The gay man is aware of this situation, but the women do not have the slightest idea that their lives are in danger. This is why AIDS is running rampant in our communities.

To appear that he is directly considering himself as a "Gay" individual, "Brother Lovelady", pretends that he is

43

approaching this game as a "Player" who plays the gay boys for what he wants. He makes request from the gay man that he finds, to purchase things that he is in need of. For example, he needs a new suit or a new pair of shoes. The gay person who is now involved with him is on a buy now, pay and play later plan. Now "Brother Lovelady" is considering himself as playing the woman's role and feels as though he is equal if not greater than the women who are in "his" man's life. "Brother Lovelady" tries to purchase expensive items that the woman will recognize right off the top and start to feel as though there is another woman in her man's life. Little does she know that she is sharing "Brother Lovelady" and he is being paid to perform sexual acts that are pleasing his ego and quenching his thirst for playing both ends against the middle. Although the Undercover Man started off as being paid not played, and originally started out creeping, he has now slipped into darkness. Sad but true, the woman has now been replaced by another man as if being replaced by a women would not hurt worse.

The Bible says, "What does it profit a man to gain the world and lose his soul?" The gay man, "Brother Lovelady" now takes full control although the "straight" man, who is the undercover man, may remain at home with his family. The woman in his life begins to feel a major void and the sex life she once shared with her man has been totally destroyed. Nothing she does will please the Undercover Man now, simply because she does not know what all it will take. In addition, the Undercover Man had already been to the mountaintop and obviously never came down. She tries to go overboard with sexual acts to make him feel as though she is just as qualified as the man who has now become a third invisible wheel. Finally, she realizes that it is totally impossible for her to be "every woman and every man" as well.

Due to the fact, this adds extra pressure to an already uptight situation, she eventually decides to go her way and let her man go his. This problem is the straw that breaks the camel's back. Friends and family will never understand what took place and the woman feels as though it is extremely embarrassing that a man took her so-called man and will live with the guilt of fighting a losing battle.

The "full fledged gay man" may be found arguing with other men about who has ownership of them while talking extremely loud. He is better known as a red-hot "flaming fag" because he does not care who knows what he is all about. He plans hot dates with his lover. They even go as far as dressing in the same colors at some point. They go on fancy trips together and take their animals along because "Tootsie" (the house cat), cannot be left in the house overnight. These lovers kiss, hug, and show affection in public. Sometimes they are holding hands as they walk through the park. They tell private jokes about funny things that happened while they made love. When out in public bars, they may be found glancing over at your man making suggestive gestures.

Older gay men, who know the ropes, know what it requires gay men to keep a certain appearance, (not too fat, not too thin, etc.)

They are also aware of the rules to the game. The older gay men play the game in a more mature fashion. The major rule is "secrets are kept just that, secrets."

I Don't Want To Grow Up

This man can be found in public listening to his mp3 player, while playing his music extremely loud and humming to the beat. So loud, that you may be able to hear the song and the radio station he is listening to, word for word. If an ambulance were to come by with the sirens on, he would not know it.

This man loves to do teenage things. He never had a chance to grow up completely. He owns every baseball cap on the market and wears it turned backwards or cocked to the side. He does not own a decent suit and usually can be found in casual clothes, tennis shoes, jogging suits and colored undershirts instead of a pressed shirt. Normally, he has no dreams or goals. He has very low self-esteem. He will spend his entire check, in order to keep up with the trends.

If he has time for a woman in his life, he generally uses her as if he were a leech sucking blood from a dog. His idea of a hot date is a six-pack, a pizza, and Freddy Krueger retrospective on DVD. The thought of going to a famous restaurant with real napkins and mousse on the menu is tantamount to winning the lottery.

Men and Child Support

This section will be short and to the point. If you are a man and you are taking care of your children, I commend you. If you are taking care of someone's children other than your own, I commend you. On the other hand, if you are not taking care of your children, the Bible says you are less than an infidel, (I Timothy 5:8 KJV) "But if any provide not for his own, and specially for those of his own house, he hath denied the faith, and is worse than an infidel." If you are a man and you are not sure if the child/children are yours, come out of denial, and get a blood test to make sure you are the father.

Trying to trap a man by having his babies is a trick as old as back in the Bible days. It didn't work in the Book of Genesis in Chapter 29 with Leah and her sister Rachel and it still doesn't work!

This is extremely important, especially since some women have been known to try to use children as a tool to make your life miserable. The next instruction is for the ladies…stop sleeping with men you are not willing to share your life with especially if you have a child/children in command. Make sure that your goal is to create a healthy environment for the child/children to live and learn in. Stop making the child feel as though he/she was a mistake. Ladies…stop taking your personal problems out on your children even if they remind you of their fathers.

We as women are strong. We are survivors. If you are taking care of your child/children and now find yourself a single mother, continue to handle your business. Anything you receive from their father will be in addition to what you already have. Contact your local child support system and find out how to go about receiving child support legally instead of making special arrangements for items you need for your child. If you are receiving child support already, please keep in mind that you should use the funds wisely.

The Mad Search for a Job

This particular person works on the lowest level of employment due to the fact that, he has not been sufficiently trained and/or educated. He may constantly let you know that he does not plan on working for a small amount of money. If the job does not pay at least $50,000.00 or more per year, he would rather wait until he can find a job in that range.

However, he may soon find himself caught up in the system, which is designed for his failure. Normally, he has a complex because the woman in his life makes more money than he does. He allows this fact to create a major problem in their relationship. Due to the fact that, most men feel as though money gives them enormous power, he finds himself extremely frustrated. Once he becomes devastated, he may begin to cause his own injuries in order to discontinue seeking employment. Such things as breaking his arm while playing basketball with the fellas, or twisting his ankle in order to have his leg propped up for two or more days. This process allows him to have an excuse for not looking for a job instead of facing the music, and approaching the issue from another perspective. Such as, but not limited to, getting a better education in order for him to be marketable and/or not losing hope and focusing on the whole picture. It would be wise for him to think positive and to discard the negative approach. This can be done, by working on the way he describes himself and refers to himself, for he is somebody.

Mr. Self Employed

Although it is possible to run a successful business as a man, it is also possible to live out a fantasy of owning your own successful business.

You have seen him before, several times. He is well known, for passing out business cards for a company of which he is the owner, operator, secretary, treasurer, president and vice president. He talks constantly about himself and all the things he has achieved during his lifetime. He may have been employed by a well-known company at one time, (where he made $30,000-$40,000 or more), and simply lost his job and decided to go out on his own. This is all well and good, however, his company has been in the red for some time and he still is not facing the realization that he should start to look for full time employment again.

His conversation is limited due to the fact, it is always based on him. After talking with this character over a drink and/ or over the telephone, you have completed a conversation where you have been allowed to say a grand total of one to two words about yourself.

He likes L.A., the Bahamas, Europe, and possibly Africa. He speaks constantly on the last trip he took to one or more of these places. The truth of the matter is he recently returned from a trip to Alabama, or the beach he said he was stretched out on over the weekend, was really at his neighbor's backyard pool.

Baby, I'm Homeless

This man will come to your house simply for a date and has no intention of leaving. You do not realize that he has moved in with you, until you have looked at this man for two or more years straight. The solution to this problem is one or more of the following. Never leave him at your home while you run to the corner store. Never make dinner and invite him to stay for a drink. Never let him lay across your bed simply to take a nap. Never fix him breakfast in bed or a hamburger the same way his mother used to. Never throw your legs behind your head while making love to him, and do not allow him to perform oral sex on you or vice versa. Never let him change clothes at your house or leave anything-not even a sock. Never do his laundry, unless it is at a local laundry mat. Never let him answer your telephone or your door. Never leave him with your children while you run across town to visit with your girlfriend. Never introduce him to your parents because he feels that gives him clout. Never let him clean, mop or take out your garbage; last but not least, never say never. Due to the fact, that a man of this nature can creep in on you with your eyes wide open. In addition, never let him cook dinner at your house and have it waiting for you when you get home. Never let him fix your beat up and broken down car...pay someone. Do not get caught feeling sorry for this individual, especially since he is a man and only the strong survive.

It is important to focus responsibility for ourselves on ourselves, rather than on someone else. If you have not been taught to do this while you were growing up, then doing it late in life can seem overwhelming at times. Learning to depend on one's self is part of re-parenting yourself and coming to realize your value as a human being

– no conditions attached. What you are able to do for yourself influences your choices about who you will depend on and for what reasons. This includes knowing that we can fall back on ourselves to meet our needs when that becomes necessary. The myth, that taking care of one's self first, as being selfish, needs to be dispelled. It should be encouraged that this process is only a means of giving yourself enough, so that you have the energy needed to care for others, if, and when you chose to do so; instead of getting caught up in a situation you will regret. In addition, it might not be a bad idea to suggest that he spend at least one night outside to see what the true meaning of homelessness is.

"Once the door of abuse opens, it never closes."
Alan D. Washington

The Woman Beater

Seventy-five percent of men in treatment for alcoholism, report acts of spousal violence. Seventy percent of domestically violent men abuse alcohol either during violent episodes or chronically. Violence is a product of the person, the situation and the effect of drugs, (if any). Violence is not caused by alcohol or other drugs. The responsibility for violent behavior resides within the individual. The choice to use alcohol or other drugs is a choice to put yourself at risk.

The way we treat others is a reflection of the way we feel about ourselves. Each time we hurt another person, our actions, negatively, affect our sense of self.

"Baby, I'm doing this to let you know that I love you." This man feels that the system used for children (discipline), will work on his woman; the "beat them and they won't die" concept. This behavior, usually happens on a lightweight basis until he gets comfortable with the way it feels to him. Suddenly, one day, you end up getting seriously hurt – even to the extent of black eyes, broken ribs, etc.

Men who beat their women are considered less than a man. Although, most men who make this procedure a habit, feel as though it makes them even more of a man. They may suggest sexual acts after beating you to make sure you know who is in control. I personally feel that pain and pleasure do not mix.

This type of man should seek professional help and start to take action on how to go about changing his behavior as soon as possible.

Normally, the children involved in this environment will end up feeling totally confused. If it is a boy child, more than likely, he will demonstrate this same behavioral pattern later in life. If it is a girl child, she will think this is the way she should be treated, and search continuously throughout her life for the same type of man. Therefore, there is a strong possibility that this behavior could end up becoming a very vicious cycle in relationships.

"There are things that we never want to let go of, people we never want to leave behind. But keep in mind that letting go isn't the end of the world, it's the beginning of a new life."

Unknown Author

The Street Life - The Dope Man

His Blackberry will go off in the middle of making love and he will get up and tell you, "Baby, I've got to make a quick move. I'm on my way to a mission." He uses your name to obtain big, fine cars and will ride other women in them. When he eventually goes to jail, you are stuck with all of his outstanding bills. One of the major characteristics of this man is seeing him with at least five of his male friends, packed in his car as if they were a can of sardines. Another major characteristic is the fact that he has several women for which he can afford, due to the fact that, he is making fast money. He lives in the fast lane.

This man is usually a low educated man who has the same needs and desires as the working man. He has decided to remedy his problems by slinging dope. Although, he knows that drugs are one of the main ingredients in killing and destroying our nation, he still accomplished 90% of his goals with this income.

Most woman envy the first lady of this type of man, since she feels she has more money, more jewelry and a more interesting and unpredictable life style.

Life in the fast lane was my initial choice. I met Karl via an associate of mine who felt I needed a man who could take good care of me and my children; for which Karl did an excellent job. I would need Karl in the worst way since Courtney had passed recently. Courtney was a man of the streets and "in the know" as well, who had just lost his life recently due to a bad drug deal. Karl was the mastermind of a major heroin ring in my city. After getting to know Karl well after building his trust in me, he decided that since I didn't do drugs nor did I drink, it would be a wise business decision to give me my own territory. This was my first experience in having servants who waited on Karl and I hand and foot. The servants would make sure we had our meals each evening and anything else to make sure our lives were hassle free.

Having my own territory seemed to be a big responsibility. This would mean that I would be required to learn how to cut the product, package the product and have my own customers to deliver the product to. Although this sounded exciting in it's own way, since it would also mean that I would have more money to put in my pockets. Fast money that sounded real good. I had even decided what my specialized plates for my car would read "SNOW". Snow would represent the color of the product, yes, that would really bring in the customers I thought to myself. During my first lesson on how to cut the product, I started talking as I always do with my hands to make my point clear. As I was waving my hands back and forth, I rubbed my eye and made the mistake of putting the product in my eye. Later that evening, my eyes closed with puss forming in both of them.

During the night, it was extremely difficult to sleep. The next day, I went to the local drug store to talk to the pharmacist on duty. When he asked me to raise my sunglasses so he could see my eyes, he spoke with authority and said "Go immediately to the Emergency Room so your eyes can be treated!" Once I arrived at the Emergency Room, the staff had several questions for which I did not want to answer. Finally, the man in charge said "There are two people you should never lie to, one is your lawyer and the other is your doctor. What did you do to your eyes?" I tried to cry, but the tears would not come down. I said, I rubbed heroin in my eyes. Although they tried to treat my eyes with eyewash, it was to no avail. I was then told that I would be required to wear two patches over my eyes for the next few days. I told them that I would not be able to do that since I had children to monitor and that I had to drive back and forth to work. For the next seven days, I was partially blind. This was a wake up call, to say the least.

Needless to say, I learned my lesson; all money isn't good money. I later left that relationship. Jewelry, fine clothes, mink coats, white sandy beaches with blue water and all the money in the world were not as important as I made them out to be. Sometimes, what most people, including myself, consider to be the "good life", can cost you your life. The fast lane was not for me after all.

"You watched me as I was being formed in seclusion, as I was woven together in the dark of the womb. You saw me before I was born. Every day of my life was recorded in your book. Every moment was laid put before a single day was passed How precious are your thoughts about me. O God! They are innumerable!

Psalms 139 15-17 NLT

Mr. Bachelor...Yes, I'm Single

This man is every woman's dream. He is so much fun to be with. You wait at home for him to call. He takes you to places on the other side of town and kisses you several times in public. He wears your favorite cologne, and makes love better than you have ever had it before. You begin to live, breathe, and taste him, only to find out that he is a married and/or a taken man.

If he is trying to pretend he is an honest man and wants to make sure all the facts are presented up front, he will inform you that he is not happy in his present relationship and/or marriage. He is also in the process of getting a divorce or breaking up with someone.

After finding out that, he is married or off limits, it is almost impossible to let him go; especially since this is now a major challenge in your life to seek and conquer. Therefore, you start to cook his favorite meals and serve him his dinner in sexy nightwear, romance him as he has never been romanced before. After dinner, you run bath water, wash his back, massage his body with warm body oils and serve him his favorite mixed drink. Before he falls asleep, he tells you to wake him up no later than 2:30 a.m. You lay awake and watch him sleep. The alarm clock rings, you quickly reach over and cut the alarm off before he can hear it. You cuddle up next to him and fall asleep. When the two of you awake, it is the morning after. He jumps up, runs into the bathroom where he begins to wash your body odor off and he rushes to the door. In most cases, he is so upset he does not remember to even say goodbye.

This man considers himself to be faithful to his wife. He is more than likely a father to at least one child and does not want his child to know that he occasionally sleeps away from home. He leads a double life due to his physical needs. His body is there with you, but his mind is on the other side of town. Instead of him making the best of his choice of a wife, he is still in need of the variety, which he feels is the "spice of life". His wife, nine times out of ten is an innocent bystander who has no idea that he is looking for love outside their home. She more than likely, is a God-fearing woman and attends Church every time the Church door opens. This man has been known to call his wife by his lover's name. For this reason, he tries to date women who have the same name or he calls all his women "My Baby" or "My Boo".

In addition, he may continue to sneak and creep with you often. However, his excuses become as thick as a book. He will make dates with you and break them, constantly. Something more important always comes up as he was on his way out of the door. He may originally take you to the best hotels in order to impress you. However, the moment you let him know you are single and living in your own home and/or apartment, it suddenly becomes more convenient to make love at your place. The wining and dining is over at this point and you become extremely frustrated with this one-sided relationship.

You may go out with a few of your girlfriends only to find him in the corner in the dark whispering the same lines he gave you to another woman. He is in search of the woman who can fulfill all of his needs. More than likely, he has not found 10 of the qualifications he requires. While on this mad search, he takes off his wedding ring to mislead his victims even further. A sure sign to recognize this type of man is, when he asks for your phone number, he feels that it is fine to give you his mother's number and may even go as far as to give you his cell phone number, which he is capable of turning off and on at will.

My questions to Mr. Uncommitted - "How long is too long when introducing your lady friend as your fiancé?"

Pamelia Tyree-Carr

Mr. I'm Every Woman's Man

"Mr. I'm Every Woman's Man", does not want to be obligated to himself, let alone one woman. He has different women for different occasions; one for the movies, one for the money, one for the honey and one just for something to do. Once we are caught up all we can say is "I only meant just to wet my feet, but this man pulled me in where the waters of love run deep."

He may eventually invite all his women to come out where he plans to be for the evening and work the room while everyone sits and stares in hopes that she will be selected to be the main attraction. He dares anyone to get an attitude with him while he parades back and forth, as if he is at his own private Women's Convention. You are left sitting on a stool with your girlfriends while he makes a complete fool of himself and you. You hold back the tears until you finally make the comment "Girl, you would never understand, he really does care about me, it's just a man thing."

In reality, you are afraid to be dropped from the most wanted list to the "X" list. In addition, you are willing to share and do not want to lose this man. You are willing to do whatever it takes "by any means necessary". There is a method to your madness. While this behavior only serves to build up the man's ego, it is at the same time, tearing down your self-esteem. Self-esteem is just that, esteem of yourself! The fact is, you are shadow boxing with several invisible women and because it is impossible to be aware of their tactics, you will never win!

Since this type of man is so busy giving everyone else a "workout" in order to keep his sexual favors, gifts, and money coming in on a regular basis, he is usually extremely tired by the time he finally gets to you.

It takes a little longer for the women to realize that this man is purchased for a price that they alone will never be able to pay. They can't afford him because he only goes to the highest bidder, until someone better happens to come along. He never considers himself as being caught because he is a wanderer. He will never belong to any one woman, in particular.

This man will more than likely get loud if you confront him about what is really going on. Right in front of the other woman and/or women, he will make statements like "I don't care what you feel for me, you have no right to question me." Or, "I'm not your man and anyone else's for that matter. Don't you ever get in my face again! As a matter of fact, I'll get with you about this later, or better yet don't call me until I call you!" At this point, you are dismissed, as he walks off as if you never had any connection with him. However, all of this is simply an act for the other women involved, so that they clearly know not to do the same thing. Please note, everybody plays the fool sometimes, there are no exceptions to this rule. The game doesn't change, the players do. What's the next step? I'm glad you asked, drop that zero and wait on your hero!

You, Me and He

January - *is his mother's birthday;*

February - *Valentine's Day;*

March - *He says that's the month he normally catches a cold;*

April - *Easter;*

May - *Mother's Day;*

June - *Father's Day;*

July - *4th of July;*

August - *Is his Family Reunion;*

September - *His daughter starts school;*

October - *Men's Retreat at his Church;*

November - *Thanksgiving with his family;*

December - *Christmas and back to January again!*

"She who puts man in dog house, will soon find him in cat house."

Hal T. Lastery, Jr.

The Married Man

There are three types of men in this category. You can take your pick, Door # 1, Door #2 or Door #3. Door #1: The married, but legally separated man who, along with his wife, are making tangible moves to dissolve the marriage. Door #2: The married man who strays every now and then and has absolutely no intention of leaving his wife. And, last but not least there's Door #3: The very married man who has no intention of leaving his wife, but engages in outside relationships and leads his Mistress to believe that he will soon be ending his marriage. Soon never comes.

I personally have been involved with a married man and have now made the executive decision that as a woman it is important not to compromise. Men like toys, if you let a man play with you, they will never buy you. Life is not about pride; it is about principle. When you date a married man, you will always, always be getting another woman's leftovers, her husband's leftover time, her husband's leftover attention, and least we forget, her husband's leftover money. No matter what lies he tells you, you tell yourself, or you both tell each other, you will never be his priority. His wife will always be the tablecloth and you will always be the dishrag. No one is going to love and respect you unless you love and respect yourself! This example is also fitting for men who claim they are in a committed relationship, which you find out is not the one you are imagining is between you and him. It is important to have a healthy marriage. It is always better to be "married for life", than merely existing in a marriage "life sentence".

Hello Girlfriend

Hello Girlfriend, or maybe that's not what I should call you. Since you really don't know me and I know all about you. Let me take the time to introduce myself. We share the same interest and that's your man and sometimes mine. I guess I got caught up in this vicious circle and I am not willing to let go.

I never would have had the opportunity to meet him if we hadn't met by coincidence. The day we met, he seemed to be having a bad day and I walked over and placed a smile on his face just by listening to his small talk. Since that time, we have shared so much; his pain, his loneliness, and his kiss of love. I give him comfort, security, and a part of my life - I'm never too busy. In other words, I give him everything he misses at home.

Sometimes we end up spending the whole night in each other's arms and before we know it, we've slept the night away. I make sure he has showered each time with the same scented soap you all use at home to wash my scent away, but not my memory. I do all this more out of respect for you. I even make sure he has his favorite cologne available for his personal use. I purchased his favorite slippers, pajamas, and underwear as well. I do this just in case you were too busy to wash and place his items where he can find them.

We often meet in a small quiet hotel, just outside of town. We eat at the fancy restaurants, where he can have his favorite meal. These are our stolen moments, precious but few. I never turn my back towards him as you do. I wait as a beggar for your love scraps to fall and before the week is over Girlfriend, they do. His wish is my command and I make his life as interesting as possible. That sexy outfit you said "No, not tonight", he purchased the same one for me. Now every night is the night! He tells me that you have his body and I have his soul, but my goal is to have all of him - his mind, his body, and his soul. May the best woman win is my method to the madness and may he go to the highest bidder - more than likely that will eventually be me. I hate spending cold nights alone and holidays too, but I welcome him with open arms - I never complain.

I often question why he is still with you while I'm alone, but I know he loves me, dreams about me, and want to be with me. He says it's because of the kids that he can't leave just yet - so I wait patiently. I realize that I can't compete with your history, but if you were to say "He's mine, leave him alone, could I? Could I find a man of my own? One without ties, one who would love me and be with me forever? I could, but even though you hold his body at night, I am always on his mind and forever in his heart and that's enough for me.

Maybe we can find the time to chat and get to know each other better at a later date. Until we meet, my suggestion to you Girlfriend would be to make your house a home and stop giving our man a reason to leave and to come to the comfort of Delilah's lap!

Signed, You, Me and He
Copyright 2004 (By Pamelia Tyree-Carr)

"Food for thought - If you win the heart of a married man and he decides to leave his wife; will he ever cheat on you?"

Pamelia Tyree-Carr

Mr. Loverman...the Smooth Operator

You knew he was trouble the moment you laid eyes on him. He may have told you about the others, and that you were just one of several women who are on his speed dial. Armed with your love, devotion and down-home cooking, you set out to change him. You were determined to make him a one-woman man for good by any means necessary.

Men who have a stable of women are not interested in settling down. For them, settling down is too scary...emotionally. Men like this, will give you a grand total of 2% of their time. You will find yourself running behind him as if he was your god. You will give him 10% of your time, but won't pay God 10% of your tithes. Maybe we have made the mistake of making men our God.

I can remember clearly a situation when one of my girlfriends called up one of her girlfriends to let her know "Hey lady, your man is cheating on us!" Although I laughed at the time, it was really a horrible situation, especially when her response was, "How can he do that to us?" Some women get involved in these Heartbreak Hotel situations, because for some reason we do not feel worthy of having our own man. Love triangles are extremely dangerous within themselves, let alone when one of the individuals involved decides to bring in the fourth party. In most cases, no one knows about the additional people being involved unless one gets caught. When is enough, enough? What is the world coming to?

The Ex-Man

Let us talk about the "Ex-Man". You can't live with him, and you can't stand to hear that he's doing well with someone else. We go back and forth to familiar doors because we feel we know what he will do. One way to stay clear of returning to this kind of situation is to stop, look and listen to your heart. Your heart is like a storage area that can recall information. If you look at the situation clearly, more than likely you will remember why you left this nutty buddy in the first place. Don't just think of all the good times, think of the good and bad things as well. Make a list of the pros and cons. My question is, "How can you expect God to send you a real man when you continue to settle for Bozo?" God wants to take you to the next level which you deserve and that is to Boaz?

Men and Their Best Friends

The main rule of thumb for this type man is to remember that, when his true friends call, he will answer! It is impossible to be all the things your man needs and, he definitely needs his best friends. This allows him to keep in touch with the outside world, in case of extreme emergencies.

His friends may tease him and remind him often that being a married man/committed man is ancient. They also remind him of the good old days when he had more women than the law allowed. His friends may not be in a relationship with anyone at this point. They want their friend back; misery loves company. More than likely, the truth is, he is not all that committed in the first place, but it sure sounds good.

Some women feel that they will have to learn to share their man with his friends or be lonely for the rest of their lives. In some cases, this man will have other male family members who are also his best friends. This family member may even make up places for them to go and find fictitious things for them to do in order to keep arguments and confusion in your home. When your man comes in late, he will claim he was out with Cousin Wilbert and/or choose to stand on the Fifth Amendment, just to keep you guessing.

Men must feel as if they are still in control of their own lives and that they do not appear to be hen pecked to their friends. Men must also feel as though they still have the relationships they were taught to have when they were children. Boys were taught not to play with girls, but with other boys only. For example, they grow up throwing rocks, playing marbles, riding bikes and playing with toy sports cars with their friends. Then they grow up from boys to men and play basketball, football and other sports, get motorcycles, purchase real cars and visit strip clubs and may even get a lap dance or two while they are there with their male friends. Please keep in mind that a night out with the boys does not necessarily mean they are cheating on you with another woman. In other words, when they were children they acted like children. Now that they are men, ain't nothing changed. They will continue to play until the day they die.

Men and Your Best Friends

"They smile in your face, all the time they want to take your place, the backstabbers." These are the lyrics to a popular song. Women need to learn the "Don't Touch/Off Limits" rule, men do as well. I have personally been in tight situations where I was forced to make an executive decision as to whether or not I should let a man come between my friend and I. I must admit, sometimes it was a hard decision to make. However, the wise choice is just to remember your values and to just say no and mean it. No is a powerful word. Why temp temptation?

Rule #1 for Women: Stop sharing your girlfriend's secrets that she shared with you, with your man. It stirs his interest in your girlfriend and makes her his private fantasy. Stop telling her things like what colors he likes, how he enjoys you in bed, where his favorite restaurant is and etc. She will have all the keys to your relationship and may one day decide to use them.

I can recall at least two instances where I made the drastic mistake of appearing to be too casual in my relationships around two women who tried to make up for my shortcomings. One instance happened when I was in a car with a male friend of mine and suggested that my girlfriend sit in the front seat while I took a nap. When I woke up, she was giving him her phone number. A few weeks later, I arrived at her home for a party she had planned for one of her children and he answered the door. Another instance was when I had a house with lots of landscaping (anyone who knows me, knows that I am not that domestic). When I arrived home, one of my friends was laying in the grass pulling my weeds from the garden at a house that a male friend of mine purchased for my children and I.

Now I know why Aretha Franklin gave several instructions about women in her song "Doctor Feel Good". The lyrics says: "I don't want nobody always sitting around me and my man. I don't want nobody always sitting right there looking at me and that man. Be it my mother, my brother, or my sister. Would you believe I'll get up, put on some clothes, go out and help them find somebody for themselves if I can? Yes I will."

Rule #2 for Men: Men should be instructed to explore and enlarge their territory, places other than within the circle of your ladies best friends and/or associates.

Following these instructions may just save you a lot of headaches and help you to keep your close friends. The safest thing to do is to learn what makes your man tick and keep him at home if he has issues staying within the safety zone.

P.S. Keep your friends close and your enemies closer.

The Religious Man Who Has Fantasies

Before I start this chapter, I would like to say that all religious men are not out of line. God still uses men in a Church setting who truly love the Lord and are trying to walk upright in His sight, to the best of their ability. However, the man in this chapter refers to a Bible toting, large cross wearing, man who appears to be in direct contact with God. He is an individual who is highly respected by his peers and well known to the public. He is often found milking women with his eyes while shaking their hands after a spirit-filled Church service.

He is often in charge of counseling at his local Church, and his opinion is highly respected. Even the Church mother adores this man she will bake him hot apple pies and fry him the best chicken he's ever had. He often holds private conferences with the women at Church and will listen to their private secrets, especially the ones that she feels should be told to him and God alone. Through these conferences, he begins to imagine the two of them performing the same cardinal sins as described via their conversations. Initially, he gives her scriptures, which address her various issues. Later he can only imagine what the bad girls of the Bible would do. Instead of what would Jesus do, he is more focused on what he would do. Not at this point, but soon and very soon, he will put forth the effort to make his dreams became a reality.

This individual goes under the name of religion and therefore, it is embarrassing to even think of making his behavior public. Especially since everyone would think it was something the woman did to bring on his behavior. He picks and chooses the scriptures, which apply to his liking and may compare himself to David and constantly quotes the fact that David was a man after God's own heart, but yet he had faults. The woman clearly understands that her trusting nature has gotten her into this and does not know how to address the pain. In my opinion, men are men, some just have a calling and an anointing on their lives. We as women should learn to get to know men better whether they are in the Church or not. Some secrets and issues are better left to tell Jesus only. As the song says, "I must tell Jesus all of my troubles, Jesus will help me, Jesus alone." We should see some signs of his faithfulness to God. Is he a praying man, does his talk match his walk with God? If not, stop, look and listen to what God is telling you in your spirit prior to being so trusting.

In my opinion, hurt that occurs from a bad Church experience takes more time to heal. If you have been hurt by a member of your Church, please seek professional help. Do not depend on your own self-healing mechanisms. Follow the man of God as he follows Christ. If and when he ceases to follow Christ, cease following him.

Younger Men With Older Women
Younger Women With Older Men

Initially, when this man meets you, he has one or more intentions in mind, which could include, running up your major credit cards and/or draining your bank account. Due to the fact, that you cannot teach an old dog new tricks, this plan soon fails. He tells his friends, "I ain't no gold digger, but I don't mess with broke women!"

While the wool is over your eyes, you will spend up to $2,000 - $3,000 taking him on expensive trips and showing him off to your other older friends, male and female, as if you are the new Stella getting your groove back. Your motherly instinct will make you feel that you can save him. Meanwhile, you are really creating a monster. You buy all of his clothes. You make suggestions for his present lifestyle, that would make him complete. And, you do not have our eyes opened to the realistic side of him, which is, he will eventually leave you for someone his own age. His sexual skills may not be up to par, so you go on a mad mission of bringing him up to status by putting him in your personal boot camp. He is a good learner so he usually takes his newfound skills and runs back to what is more familiar to him. He looks good, smells good, walks good and talks good but he should be put back into the oven, because he is half-baked.

When there is a younger woman with an older man, there is usually lack of trust; especially when other men take notice of how beautiful his lady is. The older man does not feel as though she should have a life of her own and wants her to focus only on him and his needs. If this is allowed, her life will be soon sucked up as if it were going through a silly straw. Due to the fact that, most of them are unable to fulfill her sexual needs, he starts to replace the lack with gifts, diamonds and pearls as well as other material things. On the other hand, there are older men who still have it going on; the younger woman is in for the ride of her life. There are a lot of things that can be learned from an older man, especially one who has been around the world and back. One of the main things will be his sexual skills, which will be one of the main lessons she will carry with her for the rest of her life. There is nothing like a woman who has finally found a man who can make her feel complete and like a real woman.

Mr. Possessive

This man acts as if he is a guard in a prison, with maximum security. He wants to have total control of every move you make; but he is unwilling to give you the same privileges with his time. He wants to know every detail of every friend you have male and female, so he can find out what purpose they play in your life so he can replace them. He wants to know what time you plan to leave and what time you plan to return. He expects you to consult him about every move you make. To him you would look good as a "what not" in a china cabinet.

Recently, I had a chance to slow down long enough to have breakfast with a close friend of mine. She held her fork in one hand and her cell phone in the other the whole time we were at the restaurant. She mentioned that her new boyfriend wanted her to carry her phone with her at all times, just in case he wanted to talk with her. She said that he requested that she keep the phone in her bra so she would feel it when it vibrated just in case he called. I said to her, if that be the case, he would look good carrying his phone in his underpants just in case she called. Initially, she felt this routine was cute, but soon she realized that this was just a form of control and was extremely aggravating.

I have another friend whose husband took time to remove the door to their personal bathroom. He said that it was because he loved her so much that he wanted to watch her every move. This is also known as obsession! Are you really that into a person? What are relationships coming to?

Mr. Possessive may also do things like show up at places uninvited, which is also known as a stalking. He will not give you any personal/me time. He stops living his own life because yours is obviously more interesting. If he was a busy person when you first met him, he is now more than available and willing to interrupt your agenda. In my opinion, it is important to set rules for your relationship in the beginning that will allow you to bend, but not break.

Just Cracked
By December Rose

Copyright 2006
Used with permission

The children are hungry
The cabinets are bare.
About to lose my mind
Already lost my hair.
Lost my hair over money I never can find.
He finds so many ways to get it
Only lies left behind.
Every check that I write
Just bounces right back.
He'd sell his own momma's soul for that rock of crack.
Doesn't he know crack kills?
"Cause I'm dying inside
From his pain I suffer
Every time that he's lied.
And he's lied.
At the end of my rope
I grab MAC for the stash.
ATM eats my card
And it issues no cash.
It issues no cash
"Cause it's already spent.
None of the bills been paid
Nothing's left for the rent.
I've gotta think of something
I've gotta think fast.
There's nothing left to sell
Nothing left but my ass(ets)
That's what I'll do...I'll sell the vette
Chevette that is.

After all half of it is mine
The other half is his.
And then he says, "The car's gone
I been jacked."
He ain't lying
He's just ...cracked.

The Chemically Dependent Man

This man will sell you if you sit in one place long enough. You should stop looking for that gold chain that has been in your family for the past 30 years, he more than likely sold it. Please do not leave the title and registration to your car in the glove compartment, he will borrow the car just to go for a ride and decide to sell the car to the dope man. He has debts that you know absolutely nothing about.

I know of a situation where a man was practicing breaking into his own house to time how long it would take him to get his own television out of the window. "Dope does funny things to some people, give me a nickel, brother can you spare a dime, dope will drive some people out of their minds." You must be aware of the games people play when it comes to satisfying their drug habits and other addictions. Good, sound relationships have been completely destroyed due to addictions. Listed below are some statics regarding the use of drugs and other addictions, which I felt needed to be addressed:

Statistics

The following information is from Substance Abuse and Family Violence from the AA treatment program:

Definitions:

Substance abuse – the use of drugs and alcohol resulting in negative effects on the user's ability to function (negative effects may be small or large).

Chemical dependency – relying on alcohol or other drugs to perform tasks, get through the day, or otherwise function.

Addiction – physical or extreme psychological dependence on alcohol or other drugs.

Alcoholism – addiction to alcohol.

Statistics Regarding Relationship to Family Violence:

- 70% of domestically violent men abuse alcohol (either during violent episodes or chronically).
- 75% of men in treatment for alcoholism report acts of spousal violence.
- 50% of severely abusive fathers were found to be alcoholic.
- 50% to 90% of incest perpetrators are alcoholic or abused alcohol at the time of the episodes.

Direct effects on violence:

- Violence is a product of the person, the situation, and the effect of drugs (if any). Violence is NOT caused by alcohol or other drugs. The responsibility for violent behavior resides within the individual. The choice to use alcohol or other drugs is a choice to put yourself at risk.

- Alcohol can release pent up anger, rage, etc. by releasing inhibitions. It impairs our ability to manage feelings and understand others.

- Cocaine (particularly crack) can produce aggressive psychotic symptoms and dangerous behaviors.

- Barbiturate (downers) use and withdrawal is associated with violence, especially self-destructive behaviors.

- PCB has been linked to extreme unpredictable forms of violence.

- Amphetamine (speed) withdrawal is associated with destructive behavior. Heavy users are prone to paranoia and aggressiveness.

- Steroids, combined with alcohol or other drugs can produce unpredictable and extreme forms of violent behavior.

Remember, those of us who have problems with violence, put ourselves at increased risk every time we abuse alcohol or other drugs.

Co-dependency:

Co-dependency refers to how family members relate to other family members who are abusing alcohol or other drugs. Co-dependent spouses may find themselves over-reacting to the behaviors of their substance-abusing partners. Excessive anger, rage and abusive behavior can result. If you have a substance-abusing partner or family member, you may find yourself over-reacting with violent or controlling behavior.

Similarities Between the
Use of Drugs and the Use of Violence

People use drugs, people use violence: to control others; to manage tension (feeling); because they learned how to in their family of origin.

Keep in mind that there is a difference between abstinence and recovery.

"If you can learn from every relationship and understand how it came into your life, then no relationship needs to be remembered with regret."

Deepak Chopra, M.D.

Chapter 3

Sleeping with the Enemy

*W*hen I was in high school I often felt like the ugly duckling. I wore long dresses, thick glasses, flat shoes and sometimes bobby socks. I went to my prom with a saved man who had joined the Marines. He wore his uniform and I wore a dress with a collar up to my neck, down to the floor and long sleeves. Needless to say, my entire body was covered, all but my hands. When we took pictures, I was afraid of what my family would think since he had to pose standing behind me. I thought he might appear to be too close.

I was saved, sanctified and filled with the precious holy ghost with a mind to run on and see what the end was gonna be! I sang in the choir, the gospel choir that is, and often led my fellow classmates to Christ. I would invite several of the members of the gospel choir to my home Church to sing on various occasions. Some of them would end up joining and later finding their husbands/wives at my Church. I was on my way to heaven and so glad.

I looked saved, I walked saved and I talked saved. I always seemed to admire the boys who had a gift and talent and later married my first boyfriend from school who played in the band. He could beat the hell out of the drums and could also play at least 2-3 other instruments. He loved the Lord and attended the same kind of Church I attended (The Church of God In Christ). I later had my first-born child and we were married by the time I was 4 to 5 months pregnant. As you know, in the 70's it was unheard of to expect a child before marriage. We were young and did not know all the ins and outs of what it really meant to be in a relationship on a daily basis. This part of the story could go on and on without me getting to the main point. Look for more information in my next book (Smile).

I also wondered in the back of my mind what it would be like to have a thuggish kind of guy. So, as I walked the halls of my high school I often admired another kind of guy who we will call Rufus. There has always been a side of me that likes to live on the edge. Rufus was what I consider an outstanding student; however, he was not your regular kind of student with good grades and on his way to college. He was what I call an outstanding student simply because he was always standing outside, perhaps selling pills or other forms of drugs. He was the kind of guy who had good looks on his side and could woo any girl who walked by.

He never paid me any attention, since I was in outfits other than Boodie shorts (then called hot pants) and clothes that exposed my body in any way, form or fashion. After all, I was the choirgirl with thick glasses and curly hair that my aunt curled with a hot comb. Sexy was nowhere in sight.

Years passed and I saw Rufus at a local party center in my hometown. He was standing on the wall looking around as if he was lost. Instead he was waiting to see who he could devour. That someone was me. I switched my hot behind, hotter than Cayenne pepper over to where he was standing and tried to re-introduce myself to him. He replied "Oh yeah, I remember you from school, what is your name again?" I tried over and over to explain to him who I was. You know, the one from the gospel choir, in the typing class on the second floor, my locker was across from yours. Oh, you more than likely didn't notice me, I said. He smiled with his bright white teeth and said, "Can I have this dance?" I thought he'd never ask.

As time went on, we would meet at this same party center on every occasion we could find. There were lots of activities going on at this place, since it was one of the hottest places to find just what you were looking for. They sponsored after work parties, night flights that started at 12:00 a.m. in the morning and lasted until 4:00 a.m., card nights and they might as well have had meat market nights since this was the place to find love and lust too.

Rufus and I talked on the phone a lot after we left the party center. We later decided to date each other on a more serious note. I learned from this relationship that if you are not careful, you just might get what you are asking for.

He gave me the nickname "Pebbles". I thought that was so cute. I wanted to feel as though I was in love and wanted a man to admire what I felt I had become, after the ugly duckling stage of my life. Some of my family members had given me the nickname "Auntie Sexy" and I started to walk in that name. Every outfit I wore in public signified that I felt sexy, including but not limited to the nightgowns I selected to win men over. Sexy, sexy, sexy is all I could hear in my head, because what you think is what you can become. Becoming the Proverbs 31 woman was not on my agenda. Becoming one of the bad girls of the Bible was.

Rufus and I became more than friends, but lovers. We would find places to keep our love life exciting. Places that were not necessary always in the bedroom. We would take long rides. We laughed a lot about things that would not necessarily be funny to other people. We had our own personal jokes. I met his family and he met mine. I fell in love with his mother and he fell in love with my three children. He had children as well and I would take time to take them shopping and buy nice things for them when I bought things for my children.

Rufus loved to dance and so did I. We would arrive at the party center together on several occasions and watch the other people he had dated and I had dated watch us with envy. We would sometimes wear the same colors to really make others watch us as we danced the night away on the dance floor.

Rufus said he was self-employed. That gave us a lot of time to spend together, since his schedule was more flexible than mine. I worked a job and could not wait to get to his house after work. Sometimes, I'd high tail my self over there before reporting in at home. By the way, did I mention that I was living with an older man at that time as well?

Rufus kept his regular lifestyle of chasing me and all his other women, while I chased him. I went off on the women I would catch him with and even mail nasty letters to their homes once I found out where they lived. Meanwhile, I would make up excuses why I was getting in later and later to the man I lived with, who by the way was a good man. After a while, Rufus decided that he no longer wanted to share me with the older man and he also demanded that I get rid of him within the next few days, or else I would see another side of him. Meanwhile, Rufus continued to show signs that he had not planned to get rid of his stable of women. I started to buck the system. I refused to leave the older man alone since he was the one taking care of me and my children. He was also the owner of the car I would leave with Rufus during the day. He would ride around all day in it and pick me after work.

The rude awakening was that more than likely, he was riding other women around in my car acting as if it were his. Later, I found out that Rufus had plenty of time on his hands since he was not self-employed and had not intended on finding work. In his tiny brain or in his mind, his job was to watch over me and lead me in the right direction. According to him, that was his full-time job! The other rude awakening was Rufus did not have valid driver's license nor insurance. What was I thinking?

Rufus later decided that his most important assignment was being my friend by day and my lover by night. He kept the women who he felt could supply his need of cigarettes, a daily newspaper and a bus pass, just in case my car was not available. He was able to get new outfits from the other women, as needed in order to appear to have his life in order. He was living in a two family house that his mother owned and allowed him to live in the upper portion for a total of $0 per month. What did he need a job for? He had a fully furnished apartment, with nice furniture. He had a nice place to lay his head. His mother cooked for him daily and all of the women including me would pay for his entertainment. We paid his way in to the party centers when he wanted to go out for a night on the town. When I started to wake up from this madness, I started to add up how much I was donating to the cause, which totaled over $1,500 a year for just three items. My mindset was, that it wasn't much in exchange for all the loving and fun things we planned each week. Little did I know, that there was a greater price to pay later in the relationship. When I started to complain and I refused to donate to the Rufus Fund any longer, he started to get angry every now and then and raise his voice during what I would consider just a regular conversation. Although he never hit me like the other women and his mother had mentioned to me over time, he still appeared to be an angry man.

I stayed in the relationship with both men for a long while. I felt each of them served a major purpose in my life. What more could I ask for? In my mind, I had heaven right here on earth. Now that I can see clearly, it was more like hell. Both men were excellent lovers, however, one fed my need for love and one fed my need for lust. One met my financial needs and one met my need to have a thug in my life. Rufus refused to leave his additional relationships and I was not about to ruin my good thing. I was in control of my life, no one else was.

One afternoon after I got off my job at one of my hometown's leading banking industries. Rufus called and said he wanted to see me as soon as I could get to his house. I was so excited, he needed to see me. Adorned with my business suit and my wonderful new piece of lingerie underneath, I went right over. He suggested that we take a ride since riding around the city was one of my favorite things to do as an activity. I got out to kiss him hello and he kissed me back. I was in hopes that the wet kiss would lead to an afternoon delight.

He then asked for the keys since he wanted to do the driving. Good suggestion I thought, since I had worked all day. He asked had I had anything to eat yet. I said, no. He asked where would I like to go, down by the lake or just ride around up and down the street. I said, not by the lake, let's just ride. He asked who knew I was with him. I replied, my oldest daughter. I was taught to always tell someone where you're going in case they have to reach you. He asked again who knew I was with him and I gave the same response. As we rode throughout the city, I was thinking about how good it felt to be with him and how I couldn't think of a faster route to get to him after I got off work. I was thinking about the good love that awaited me as soon as we got back to his house.

Rufus drove for several hours back and forth. Finally, he pulled me to a street that did not have proper lighting and asked me again, who knew I was with him. He then asked what did I decide to do about the older man I lived with. He said he was in hopes that I had decided to choose him instead of the older man. So, being the kind of person I am, always telling jokes I replied, "I'll let him go when you decide to let all your whores go." as I started to laugh.

Rufus did not respond to my laughter as he normally would. Instead, he pulled a pistol out and put it to the left side of my head and said, "It really doesn't matter who is aware that I am with you, because I'm gonna kill you and possibly myself. I asked you to choose and since you haven't done that fast enough, I'll choose for you." I wanted to cry but I could hear the voice of God telling me not to show any emotion. I felt a tear fall from my right eye instead of the side he could see.

Rufus then took the pistol from the side of my head and continued to tell me how he felt about me, how much he loved and needed me and how he did not have any intentions of sharing me any longer. He then put the pistol back to my head as I pleaded with him not to pull the trigger, especially since I had children and so did he. I reminded him that we both had people who loved both of us. This really did not seem to matter to him for what seemed to be a very long period of time. I learned what prayer really means as I started to pray within my spirit. God does hear a sinner's prayer after all.

Needless to say, Rufus finally took my suggestions and started to drive off back toward his house. I was afraid not to go inside when he did, so I joined him. He promised never to do any such thing again and asked me to forgive him. He even had the nerve to kiss me as he normally did with hopes that I would stay for the night to make love to him. After leaving that evening, I decided to change my wicked ways and learn to be content and to love the man I was with. It's important to know who you are as well as who's you are. You were bought with a price. Before you entered into your mother's womb God knew you and gave you a divine design before you arrived. As my aunt says to me often "Pamelia, you are somebody!" Whether you are ugly, blind, crippled or crazy, learn to know who you are! We as women are often looking for love in the wrong places, with the wrong people. We sometimes even look thirsty. Thirsty for love and affection; hoping to feel complete and wanting to be needed.

Rufus later was given a 15-30 year sentence for abusing one of his children's mother. That did not last long however, since he was later released for good behavior. As a matter of fact, I was shocked to see him standing in line at my father's funeral. He leaned over and whispered in my ear "Hello Pebbles." I almost joined my father to say to the least.

"Never complain about what you permit."
                                        Author Unknown

It Is No Mystery

Recently, I stopped to ask myself what messages or signals was I giving off that kept drawing mostly negative relationships towards me? Did I appear to be needy, selfish, suffering from low-self esteem, hopeless, insecure, arrogant, fearful, angry, frustrated, and lonely, in need of sexual healing or just plain stupid? In my mind, I am none of these. In my mind, I am whole and very sure of myself.

After years of not getting it right, I thought I would stop to consider what real love looks and feels like. It definitely is not music playing, flowers blooming, and birds singing while making love. True love must make you feel whole and complete and will also allow you to trust an individual with your heart and soul.

In most cases, I felt as if I was in a vicious cycle, which never ended, while continually riding looking for love, which in turn kept me from arriving at contentment.

While holding a serious conversation with a friend of mine, a while ago, "It is no mystery" was his answer to a question that I felt held a lot of weight. It is no mystery, ain't that about nothing! This was his response to my question as to where did I fit into his busy schedule. In other words, he reversed the questions on me, which really meant, can't you see I've been too busy to be concerned about our relationship?

In my opinion, when a man feels that his relationship with you is not a top priority, is when it's time for you to stop and re-evaluate where you think the relationship is really going. I feel, more than likely, the relationship is going nowhere. This is when you should change your wish list into a real list with questions like: Is it time for me to move on? What would I lose if I moved on? What will I gain if I stay? Is my mental, physical and/or financial status going to change? If a change takes place, will it be for my good? Life in general is really no mystery. I have often heard people say, "There's nothing permanent in life but change." Change can be a good thing, if you stop long enough to see the warning signs.

"Those who do not respect your assignment disqualify themselves for a relationship."

Author Unknown

Who Stole My Microwave?

One hot summer night, as the sun was going down, I stopped in the Church parking lot after a wonderful revival. There stood a good-looking man who I later found out went by the name of Stevenson. Stevenson had on a wonderful outfit with the hat and matching band to boot. He smiled at me and we started to walk towards each other. A close friend of mine noticed the attraction and started to walk towards us. My friend introduced us as we continued to stand in the parking lot and later decided to leave and go out for a bite to eat.

Wow, was all I could say after the good conversation during our meal. Stevenson and I stopped long enough to exchange phone numbers. Since he was just arriving back to the city, I felt it was my personal duty to make sure he had a chance to reacquaint himself with the new places to go and things to do. After all, what harm would it be to become his personal escort? After going out on dates with him here and there, I decided to cook him a home cooked meal with the candles and all the other accessories in order to make a fun-filled evening. This time together would allow us to get to know each other better. He ate the dinner I prepared for him, we sat and talked for a while and then he kissed me good night as he left. I thought to myself, "He's such a gentleman. He even left before midnight. He will more than likely be a good catch."

Stevenson, drove a nice Jag, which had a drop top. He looked good, smelled good, and he even had fresh breath. My, his stock looks pretty good to me. He had the ability to quote scriptures and felt he had a calling on his life to one day become an Elder in the Church.

The next day, when I arrived home I noticed that the lock to my apartment door did not turn properly. I then asked the gentleman who lived in the apartment building had he noticed any unusual activity while I was away. He said, yes, he saw a gentlemen there earlier in the day, who was in a nice white car. He also mentioned that he didn't think much of it since he saw the car there the night before.

I entered the apartment with much caution, since I really was not sure what was going on. Once I was inside, I noticed that someone had taken a nice hot shower and that my microwave oven (that my grandparents bought me for a gift) was now gone. In addition to that, there was a nice crisp white shirt lying across my bed, just like the one Stevenson had on the night before. Stevenson had taken time to break into my personal space. Later, I found out that Stevenson had arrived back in town not necessarily by choice. He had done someone wrong on the West coast so he had to return to the north end of the world. Stevenson was a professional con man! Is that the only part he forgot to tell me over dinner?

Lesson: Everything that looks like pure gold, might just be 14K dipped in gold. In other words, stop being so trusting. Learn to look within the individual to see where his heart really is.

Thief in The Night

A close friend of mine suggested that a close friend of his should drop my car off to him since he needed a car to get around to take care of some important business. His friend was a well-dressed individual, who was tall and handsome and wore his head shaved. With no thought, I gave his friend the keys to my car so it would be easier for my friend to start off on his mission. I instructed my friend to call me once his friend arrived. Later that evening, I still had not heard from my friend. He later told me that he was under the impression I never gave the keys to his friend. Three days later, neither of us had heard from him. I began to beg different people to pick me up to go to and from work and even had to buy bus tickets and started catching the bus.

By this point, I was so angry; not just at my friend but at myself as well. How dumb could I be? I did not know this man well enough to give him the keys to my car. Was I that desperate for a new friend that I was willing to lose such a valuable possession as my car? When one of my friends from middle school heard about the situation, the first thing she suggested was that we start looking for the car ourselves. We decided to check in an area where drugs were sold, just in case he had sold the car for drugs.

I called someone who knew about the streets and asked him who was running the drug area on the east side of the city. He mentioned the man's name and off we went with two guns, in case we had to let the ghetto out of us. We went off to the area, two women who looked like Pistol Toting Annie's. When we arrived, the man in charge of the area stepped out of the crowd and thought it was amazing that we had the nerves to come in a drug-infested area with guns. He made mention that he did have my car and the only thing that was wrong was he had used all the gas and removed my CD player. He had us follow him to his house and returned the car back to me.

Lesson: Never trust anyone with items they cannot replace. Do not let an individual's looks fool you. Men who are well dressed can also have drug problems. Never date a man who needs to borrow your car; especially when you do not know him well enough to know the places he hangs out at. Last, but not least, men should never underestimate the power of a woman! After all, most women know how to investigate you as if they were employees of the CIA (Central Intelligence Agency), the ATF (Alcohol, Tobacco and Firearms) and/or the FBI (Federal Bureau of Investigation). Let's not forget Pipl.com where you can investigate anyone via the computer. In other words, there is nowhere to run and no place to hide if a woman really wants to find you.

"There's a Hole in my Sidewalk"
by Portia Nelson

Chapter 1.

I walk down the street.
There is a deep hole in the sidewalk.
I fall in.
I am lost…
I am helpless.
It isn't my fault.
It takes forever to find a way out.

Chapter 2.

I walk down the same street.
There is a deep hole in the sidewalk.
I pretend I don't see it.
I fall in again.
I can't believe I am in this same place.
But it isn't my fault.
It still takes a long time to get out.

Chapter 3.

I walk down the same street.
There is a deep hole in the sidewalk.
I see it is there.
I still fall in… it's a habit.
But, my eyes are open.
I know where I am.
It is my fault.
I get out immediately.

Chapter 4.

I walk down the same street.
There is a deep hole in the sidewalk.
I walk around it.

Chapter 5.

I walk down another street.

"Loneliness is not the absence of affection, but the absence of direction."

Author Unknown

"What you can tolerate you cannot change."
Author Unknown

"Celebrate every relationship you've ever had. For better or worse, your relationships are your best teachers."

Christine Northrup, M.D.

Chapter 4

Pack Light

"Casting all your cares upon him; for he careth for you." -
1 Peter 5:7 (KJV)

Recently, I had to take a trip to California to attend my aunt's funeral. I stayed up most of the night because my flight was scheduled to leave at 5:55 a.m. from a nearby city, which would take approximately one hour to get to. This would mean that I would be required to leave home no later than 4:00 a.m. in order to arrive on time. Initially, I had placed several items in an extra large bag with my clothing laying in the bag in no certain order. A close friend of mine noticed the large bag and decided to repack the items into two bags. Needless to say, this did appear to be a better idea.

Once I arrived at the airport, I tried to drag the items to the counter so they could be checked in. This process would take much longer than I planned. Especially since eight other individuals had the same idea as I did. By this point, the process took so long that I missed my flight by ten minutes. I started to cry uncontrollably and the attendant noticed my frustration and rescheduled me on the next flight as a stand-by. This would now cost me an additional $50.00.

On my way to the security check area I could barely make it with both bags. Once I arrived at the security area another attendant made the comment "Sistah, you need luggage with wheels. You will never make it like that." I started to cry again once the attendant started making several request, ones like: "Please remove your jacket; take off your shoes and remove your jewelry." They continued with questions like: "Do you have any liquid substances in your bag?" At this point, I thought they would eventually ask if anyone in line had false teeth, if so, please remove

114

them prior to approaching this area. In other words, the questions went on and on.

After being finally being to move on to the next level, and feeling totally exposed, the same attendant approached me again. He then said "I've watched you struggling with your bags, let me help you", as he strapped the two bags together so I could make it. I then told him how frustrated and unbalanced I felt and how I had missed my initial flight. Now, there were no seats left on the re-scheduled flight, which caused me to be instructed to go back to the initial starting point. Tears began to flow once again. I thought to myself, this is the trip from hell, I may never make it in time for the funeral at this rate.

Back through security I went with the same procedures all over again. But this time, things would be different. I checked my luggage in with the attendant at the cost of $60.00 for two bags. What would have been a 20 minute process lasted hours (just like Moses trying to get to the Promise Land).

This time when the attendant saw me, he asked "What did you do with your bags?" I replied, "I had enough sense to check them in this time. I learned how to pack light."

The moral of the story is: Do not allow life to cause you to continue to hold on to things you should let go of. Do not carry unnecessary hurt, pain, abuse or people who may never truly love you. Stay away from emotionally destructive and toxic relationships. Do not carry other people's issues and/or any unnecessary weight that can easily beset you. When God assigns someone to help you, let them and do not be ashamed to admit you need help. Follow instructions first time given or you may

115

be required to repeat the lesson. Expect better things to come your way the second time around. Your latter will be greater than your past.

This chapter is dedicated to the security attendant at the airport who recognized I was a Sistah in trouble, who needed his assistance in the worst way. When I mentioned to him that I was in the process of writing a book titled, "If He Ain't Mr. Right, He's Mr. Wrong", his comment was "What if a man is both of them?" Good question. This shot out goes to Minister Timothy R. Morrow, Sr. better known as "Big Daddy". Thanks for going the extra mile and helping a Sistah out. Minister Morrow, Sr., you taught me a good lesson and that is: If and when life causes you to repeat a lesson, pack light!

Characteristics of Mr. Right

Honest

Loyal

A Hard Worker

Good Ethics

Courageous

Punctual

Dedicated

Trustworthy

Loving

Compatible

A Gentleman

God-fearing

Provider

Pure

Teachable

Whole

Surrendered

Forgiving

Not a dream killer

Ask yourself does this person seek God willingly and eagerly on his own? When it comes to growing spiritually, does he read the Bible, pray, and go to Church even without you? Does this person have a passion for God?

Why Settle?

I work with a lady who has the following license plate "YSettl". When I pass by her truck, I stop and look each time and ask myself the same question, "Why settle?" I have talked with several women who feel they must have at least one "thug" experience in order to complete who they are. My response to them is, just because no one has shown up that can love them on their level does not mean they have to sink to someone else's level. Just because God is still preparing their King, does not mean they are not a Queen-in-waiting. They are complete. They must say to themselves, "I am not the better half, I am whole. I do not have to live as though I am not worthy of having a whole, complete relationship. I bring good things to the table of life, therefore, I am worthy of having a good one-on-one relationship and/or a wonderful marriage." So, from this day on, walk worthy!

Chapter 5

From a Man's Point of View

"Life is a value worth buying but thinking my dear friend, is the only coin noble enough to purchase it. In other word, use the brain God gave you to choose a life mate."

Walter Simpkins

Not Mr. Perfect, but Mr. Right
By Minister Aaron B. Thomas

I want to begin by saying that there is a saying I tell all people who are looking for a potential covenant candidate: "Conversation without destination is devastation." It simply means what it says: If two people connect with each other, but there is not a real destiny in the connection, then someone is headed for a real Heartbreak Hotel. I believe there are a lot of disconnections in relationships because someone refuses to have a daily "Flesh Funeral." Just think, if there can be submission in one situation, then two people can get over the situation. I once heard a man say "Never marry potential, marry reality."

I totally disagree with this philosophy. You can marry reality and it can potentially go bad, hit rock bottom, or be totally destroyed. On the other hand, you can marry potential that can move you into your desired reality because of faith, hope, prayer, and a vision. I believe if two people are serious, seek God, and WAIT on His answer without moving ahead of God, there can be a strong connection. This does not erase the test, trials, and tribulations that a covenant connection will go through, but when inviting God in, a STRONG prayer life, and obedience to God's Word on both ends, there will be divine strength in the struggle. Marriage or relationships are or can be like a rollercoaster ride; you have your ups and downs, but it is still fun.

There are three types of people I want to introduce you to. I will not point to one specific gender because you have this spirit operating in both male and female. You first have the "Scavenger" this is the one that has gathered things that have been discarded by others as a junkman.

This one is full of mess when he approaches you, but it is hidden. Then you have the "Parasite", one that draws or takes advantage of another and gives NOTHING in return, leaving you feeling drained. Then you have the "Leech". A leech is another kind of parasite that starts off a dark color (usually black, dark brown or grey) and then latches on to flesh and sucks blood and turns the color red after it feeds. Notice I said attaches to flesh. So, if you are walking in the Spirit, it cannot latch on and suck from you because it latches on to flesh.

There are some Mr. Rights as well, not Mr. Perfect, but Mr. Right who understands his role as a man who covers, contributes, caresses, and cares about your total well-being, your spiritual, emotional, mental, and physical being.

He is a team player and not a poor sport. He may not always be able to reach in his pocket and pull out money, but he is able to reach in his heart and pull out a message. He may not have all the answers, but he may have strong advice. He may not be able to lift the heaviest weights, but able to help carry some of your heaviest burdens. He may not be the knight in shining armor you fantasized about, but the one dressed in full armor that God has prepared or is preparing for you. He may not be the biggest and baddest dude you expected, but the biggest and baddest do not mess with him because he is anointed. He has done some wrong in his life, but he has been forgiven by God to earn the title to be your personal, Mr. Right.

"A strong relationship is built upon trust and hard work. It is a work in progress; you can never stop working. To get better, you have got to put work in. "

Michael Clifton

The Measure of a Man
By Desmond Pringle

It is so ironic that Pam would ask me to write a commentary on my thoughts of what is a good man. The irony is that I first met her in the early 90's as I toured the country in a gospel musical entitled, "A Good Man Is Hard to Find", and my character was the good man. My character was a hard working, honest Christian man who married a woman, adopted her son and raised him as his own, provided a stable home environment for his family and even put his bride through college. Once she graduated and became a part of corporate America, this same husband who was a successful entrepreneur started being viewed as a menial blue-collar worker. Or, as she put it, he was nothing but a dirty, greasy, nasty mechanic.

What is a good man? I believe it starts and ends with the heart of the man. Who is he at his core? What are his values? These are the kinds of questions I think a woman should ask herself and use as a gauge to rate whether or not the individual is a good man. Being a good man has nothing to do with looks, the car he drives, the house he lives in, or the places he dines. If he is an abuser, a cheater or a user, none of these external accoutrements is going to make for a healthy relationship and ultimately if the woman is desirous of a serious relationship, this will have been a waste of time. There are men who enjoy the chase, the pursuit and once they have captured they release shortly thereafter. These men are found in every arena of life. They are in the clubs, workplace, the gym, the grocery store, and yes even the Church. You cannot assume that just because you meet someone in a venue other than the nightclub and they appear to be decent that his values are going to be congruent with yours and ultimately qualify him to be a good man.

As a pastor, I will not even say that a good man is a man who loves the Lord. I know first hand that there are many men who are in Church and are not in any position to be in a healthy relationship with any woman. Because their issue(s) are not obvious, and because they are making the attempt to walk and work through those issues they appear to be prime candidates to the myriad of female parishioners believing God for their husband. What I would say to my precious sisters, not only look before you leap, but assess before progress in the pursuit of a relationship. The absolute best thing you can do is continue to work on you and be committed to being the best you - emotionally, mentally, financially spiritually, socially and otherwise. This is the portrait of the Proverbs 31 woman.

A good man is never standing idly waiting to be seen. He is busily committed to personal responsibility, self-improvement, and service to situations greater than himself. A good man is hard to find because the virtuous woman is the one who catches his attention.

A Word to the Wise is Sufficient

Sikandar Z. Hameen

First of all, let me qualify myself. I am a male that lived in a household of seven to eight women. In other words, I was raised by women. My father vacated the home when I was about two. I had a sister who was younger than I, that transitioned in 1991. Question is…how do you know a man who was raised by women? He puts the toilet seat down.

I am a Vietnam veteran and I have two children. One is early thirties and my youngest is 12 years of age. I was married 14+ years and divorced in 1985. My ex and I became very close friends. She made her transition in 2000. Now ladies and gentlemen, let us get to the meat and potatoes.

For some reason women who are in a physical and otherwise abusive relationship think that there is no way out. For example, in my hometown, we have had several highly educated women murdered by males with no or a lesser education. If it is the man who is educated and the breadwinner, he abuses from the top down. Women tend to accept this behavior because he is the educated one and the breadwinner. If it is vice versa and she is the one on top with the education and bringing home the bacon, he tends to abuse her from the bottom up.

Either they believe they can change this person or they can compromise their relationship and spiritually overcome the shortcomings in this person. How would you know that the relationship is coming to an end? The steps to the door are slow and very short, and, if you pay attention, the door is closing fast.

I will use two occasions as my example. My former wife accidentally bleached my colored clothes. Never in 14 years had she done this! Years later, the young lady that I was in a relationship with for nine years accidentally bleached a colored jacket. I do not believe it was intentional, but the relationship was unwinding due to a lack of consciousness. The door was beginning to close on our relationship. There were other little things going on in the relationship that were showing me that the relationship was stepping off to the far right. It was not about finances but we were simply growing apart from each other. Sexually I was King Kong. But, when you outgrow each other, not even finances or sexual dynamics can guarantee a smooth ride.

I love and respect women. Now there are men who are married to women; there are men who have children by women and there are men who go with women, but, they do not love a woman. This is a process that is developed from birth. Do you really love your mother? If so, you will respect, honor and not do anything that would bring shame to your family. One writer said, "My eyes adore you." To adore is another level of respecting and loving someone. Therefore, you go past love. You want to be their protector and confidant. Ladies, I know that there is a shortage of men on the planet today. The shortage is even greater because they are either dead, in prison or homosexual. So, when you go fishing, fish with the rod and not the net. When you go fishing with the rod, you put on the hook what the fish like. When you fish with the net, you do not know what you are going to catch, with the rod, you can be selective.

Be strong because you are the mothers of civilization. You are the queens of the universe. A child's first lesson is from his mother. Do not ever let anyone live in your head rent-free. When my daughter was a young adult, she and her young friend decided they wanted to get married and asked me for financial help. My response was I cannot help you right now but...if you are in love, you can wait; but if you are in heat you cannot wait. So, needless to say, they took the HEAT. In closing, be strong and be good and do not take any B. S.

With all respect and love,

The son of Mrs. Rosetta Otey
Sikandar Z. Hameen
fka Alexander M. Otey

Chapter 6

Life Stories

Compiled From Women

From all Walks of Life

There hath no temptation taken you but such as is common to man: but God is faithful, who will not suffer you to be tempted above that ye are able; but will with the temptation also make a way to escape, that ye may be able to bear it.

I Corinthians 10:13 (KJV)

A Five-Year Roller Coaster Ride

Mr. Wrong #1

"TW"

I just knew he was the one, even though he did not think so and told me as much! Yes, God always provides a way of escape. I just did not take it!

When I met TW, I had been separated from my former husband for three years. We had filed for a divorce, called it off the day before it was to happen, moved back together only to find out it was not going to work. So here I am out of $3,000, living on my own and not even thinking about the fact that I am still married. I wanted a relationship! Sounds crazy now, but back then I was truly divorced in my mind and it was only a matter of time before we would go back through the process and make it happen for real this time.

I met TW at a local sports bar. I saw him a few times when I went there. He looked very familiar...like I knew him from somewhere. One day a guy my friends and I had met introduce him to us. Nothing happen. He came to the table spoke and that was pretty much that. Weeks later, my best friend and I went there again and he was there. He came over to where we were, and he and I talked the entire evening. We exchanged numbers and he called me a couple days later. We clicked instantly. We talked on the phone quite a bit for about a week and planned our first date. Now mind you he told me he was living with a chick, but, it was just a friend. She knew his cousin and needed someone to move in, he needed a place and they set it up. (Red Flag #1)

We go out to a bar/restaurant that is in his friend's apartment complex. Now mind you the place was all-abuzz. It was packed just like a regular bar or restaurant would be. I figured wow, this place is pretty cool, he knows of some of the city's best-kept secrets. To top it off he wanted me to meet his friend. We had a nice time. He dropped me off at a decent hour. Cool. The next day, we went out again. Cool. We talked almost every night. We exchanged email addresses and would email each other throughout the day. Soon email would be our main means of communication. (Mistake #1) My sister gave him the nickname "Correspondence" because she said that all we were doing was corresponding! I did not see anything wrong with it being the email queen that I am. Besides, I was always on my computer anyway, even at work. He kept really late hours some nights in the studio as he is a local producer, so email was cool with me.

We went out a couple more times, talked on the phone and, of course, emailed during the next few weeks. Now in my mind I am thinking this is leading to a relationship. No, we never discussed it (Mistake #2), but I just knew. I shared things with him so easily, intimate, personal things that only my nearest and dearest might get to know. I thought we were truly connected. I realize you always need to know where you stand with a man. Assume nothing! Be confident to tell him up front what you want and what your standards are. Right? Yeah right.

What I also realize now is that being vulnerable, sharing and opening up is not easy for me. The fact that I was able to do that with him gave the illusion of a connection. Yeah, he is the one I thought. So what, he told me more than once, "I'm not good enough for you." So what. He's the one. So what, he told me he thought he was too selfish to be in a relationship, he was the one. I kept telling myself that off and on for five years. I saw a few other people in between, but if and when that did not work, I chalked it up to my true love for TW. Yeah, that is why nothing became of those other guys. I truly love TW, I told myself. Yeah, he is the one. If you tell yourself something enough times I guess you start to believe it!

I slept with TW six weeks after our first date. (Mistake # 3) And to be quite honest I thought I was doing something by holding out so long! When we were together it was intense and I just could not hold out any more. Now mind you, I am saved at this point in my life. I was a tithing, faithfully attending service, praying, fasting, Christian. Remember, I am also married. None of this crossed my mind. See I was not fornicating, no, I was committing adultery and it never crossed my mind! This is the relationship I was praying about for years. This is the relationship I wanted God to bless! Seems crazy now, but that is how I thought.

TW and I did not have a love affair. I kept trying to play the good girl role that just slipped. Please! I tried to make it appear like I really did not want to, but could not resist after a while. I thought by holding out, he would want me more. We probably only slept together one or two more times that year. Our dating dropped off to a minimum. I reasoned to myself that it was because he was moving into his own spot. He had a Vegas trip coming up and there was a lot going on in his life. Yeah, that was it. I tried to be supportive of all that was going on for him during the next few months. However, the year ended with us not really being any closer than we had started out in the beginning.

The following year, one of us contacted the other and that led to a few months of constant communication, hooking up and the illusion. The illusion of this time, I think we are headed for "couple-dom." This went on for the next four years after (Mistakes # 4-6). We would get back in touch with each other, talk, connect, hang out, tell each other how much we loved each other, possibly sleep together, lose touch again and repeat the same routine next year.

I did really well it seemed during even numbered years for some reason. I held to my guns and did not sleep with him. I was a praying, working out sister. And, I was not going to do it. I even presented the possibility of a sexless relationship to him. I talked about fornication with him, hoping he would see what I was talking about. Nope. He was not hearing it. Did not understand it. He told me God knows how he made us and did not want us to be miserable. I knew TW and I were not on the same page spiritually, but he was the one, right?

One night last spring TW and I were talking on the phone, it was about time for us to do our annual hook up with each other, so I thought. We talked like old buddies, best buddies. We laughed got caught up. Wondered how in the heck we got out of touch. Oh, yeah, I reminded him, I had invited him to some very important events the previous fall and he was a no show. I just knew he was coming to my Ordination. I mean that was like one of the most important days of my life. I told him as much. He had been with me through my fornication struggles. He had been with me through my transformation the last five years. And though, he was not, nor never had been my boyfriend, he was indeed a friend, a close one at that. Dude did not show!

During our last phone conversation, we talked about dating and relationships. He said that he would make a good boyfriend. HUH!? I told him I did not see that. I told him he does not make a woman feel loved. That he is not a pursuer. Anyway, we talked about one of his friends who was divorcing, relationships in general and some women he was seeing. SCREEEEECH!!! Stop the bus! I really do not want to hear this, but ok. He tells me that they are not sexually compatible. YIKES! Lord knows I did not want to know that you are sleeping with someone. He tells me it is not like us. That we are like that scene from Monster's Ball all the time, every time. It was true. When we did sleep together, it was, well let us just call it passionate. He goes on to tell me how they click and vibe and she told him that it does not matter about where he was it was about growing together as a couple.

WHAT!!!!? Haven't I been saying that same thing for five years!!!! Long story short, he tells me he thinks she might be the one! WHAT!? I thought I was, but you just were not ready. You were not good enough. But, you good enough for her, huh? How does that work?

My heart felt like it was falling out of my chest. I really got my face cracked. WOW. I could hardly talk, let alone breathe. Through the tears, I managed to tell him to work it out with her, the sex can be worked on. If he really felt she was the one, hold on to her and work it out. He kept telling me not to cry, and how bad he felt. I was a bawling idiot. I was so humiliated. I had to keep myself from crying so hard, so I hung up. I have not talked to him since.

Ishmael Ain't Isaac!
Mr. Wrong # 2 "N.C."

The enemy knows what you like and will send the decoy! Never mind the red flags, it is enough of what you want to make you shut an eye to a few red flags. Ok, so NC had the look, the Timberland boots (Tims) that I love, he pursued me tough (I love to be pursued), he was romantic, fun and a great lover! And, oh he came from a family of Christians! Though he was not all the way practicing our faith himself, I didn't have to explain fasting, tithing, why I have bottled oil next to my huge house Bible, my tambourine or anything else. He understood it all. We were on the same page I thought. He even went with me to Church! And get this, his sister and my sister are best friends! Hooray, right? Wrong. What is the matter you ask? Oh, did I fell to mention he lived with a chick? Um hmm, yeah. For ten years. Claimed he was only staying for his daughter's sake, blah, blah, blah. Then eventually claimed he was moving out blah, blah, blah. That was in "07 and as far I know, they still live together!

How did we get together? My sister, who lives out of state, came home to visit. We went out to dinner for her birthday with her best friend and some of her family. NC was there. We had met before I am sure, but I was dating, engaged or married back then and he was not around much like the rest of the family, so we really did not see each other much. I remembered him, but had forgotten how absolutely gorgeous he was! During dinner he fed me off of his plate! He was extremely attentive. So much so it was a little overwhelming and embarrassing.

I went outside for some air and he was on my heels. Now, I cannot lie, I was loving it because like I said,

I do like a man that pursues. We sat outside on a bench and he asked me about who I was seeing or dating. I told him about TW. He did not seem phased. He said, "That's not your man, so..." He told me he was moving out from his live-in girl friend. He told me how miserable they had been for last few years and how they were just trying to get their daughter to a place of understanding and get the finances together to separate. I understood that. I stayed in the house with my ex-husband for months until the end of the school year. We agreed that moving in the middle of the school year would be too much. So I got it. They were trying to handle this considerately...so I thought!

After dinner, we were going to try to find some live jazz or something that we all could do. He was holding my hand through the parking lot and insisted that I ride with him.

We went looking for live jazz, but did not like any of the places, so everyone decided to call it a night. Well, except NC and I. We dropped my sister off at my house and went back out.

We drove around a bit still in pursuit of a band or something to do. We talked and drove and eventually he brought me home. We exchange numbers and he said he would call.

And boy did he call. We talked almost every day and went out every weekend for about a month. At first, it seemed both our sisters were as pleased as punch. They commented how they saw the chemistry and how cool it was that we vibed so. His sister told me she had never seen him like this. But, I guess they soon realized his behind was not really leaving his live-in. I think both of their husbands had a hand in that. They both thought it was not a good idea. And, they were right. His sister called me and

137

told me to cut it off with him. At this point, I had not slept with him, but I really did not want to cut it off. He is moving. They will see. People who have never experienced anything like this do not get these delicate situations. That is what I told myself. The reality is my brother-in-law and his knew he was full of $#!!.

We went riding on his motorcycle, we went to the movies, we went out to eat, we were just going. We were talking, vibing, and all seemed well. And then, one day he asked to come to Church! What you say! He loved it. Uh-oh. He knows one of the pastors. Uh- oh. Suddenly, I begin thinking, this does not seem right. I was headed on vacation with my girl friends and told him I needed to think about us. He was over the night before I left. I now realized he had to make sure I thought about him while I was on vacation. We had not slept together up to that point, but that night, he was on my heels and was not taking no for an answer. He was not trying to hear about not fornicating, my call to ministry or none of that!

I decided while on vacation that I was going to call it quits with him. He had not shown me any signs of moving and it just did not feel right in my spirit. I knew it was not right, but I was getting something out of it. I was getting the attention of a very attractive man, I was being pursued, taken out and our chemistry was like outta this world. It just resonated for all to see. Everyone told us how they saw it when we were together. How we brought the best out of each other. How we seemed to glow when in each other's presence. Glow, smo he had to go!!! This ain't right, and I knew it.

When I got home I called him to come over. This man cried. When I told him I did not think I could see him any more, he cried. I felt terrible. I was so trying to

138

make the right decision. I teared up as well. But, I knew I was doing the right thing. I knew this relationship was not pleasing to God. And knowledge is not power as some say it is. No, I have a whole other spin on it. Knowledge is responsibility.

I was scheduled to have surgery about a week later. It kept me off my feet for about two to three weeks. He was Johnny-on-the-spot. He bought me flowers. He bought me popsicles. He came over to check on me. And, though I really believe he did all that to look good in front of my friends, I think he did care and it was hard to resist. Once I healed, he pressed me to go to an end of the summer cook out. I agreed and it was hard to shake him after that.

We went through most of September with me telling him I could not see him until he moved out. I did not call him. I would not answer all his calls, but the ones I did, I told him the deal. His dad got really sick and my sister suggested that I call to let him know I was praying for him and his family. Big mistake. Though I was sincerely praying, I should have just kept it at that. I did not want to appear cold though. But he is the type you cannot give an inch to. Any communication to him was a sign to press forward. By October, he was just checking on me and slowly getting back in. By November we were together all the time again and in a full fledge passionate love affair. My friends included him in my birthday plans that month. We spent Christmas Eve together. I took him with me to the two best friends" homes I normally visit. I have never taken a date to either of their homes at Christmas time except my ex-husband. It was like NC was in. Everyone commented on how he made me smile and how good we seemed together.

I felt it too. I think he did as well. One small problem…. it was five months later and he was still living with a woman! We met in July and now it's December and well, doesn't look like it's happening. I am not as sure as I was that he was indeed going to move. I am all into him now and we have been sleeping together like dogs in heat! Boy, oh boy. I have got to get a grip. Things sorta came to me after that. I was getting phone calls from a woman asking me what my relationship was to him. She did not give the live-in's name, but I am pretty sure it was her. He hung up on me one day in the middle of conversation because apparently she walked in the room. You talk about ticked. WHAT? Thought you were moving so what is with the hang up? Why do you care about being on the phone in her presence?

He still stuck to the story that he was moving. I made up my mind that by January, we would be done. He put up a good fight, but by February I had let him go. He continued to call me that summer. Talking the same lame thing. Still living with guess who? With no intentions of moving. Wow! He looked the part, was from the perfect family, was the perfect age, had swag, wore Tims, knew the Lord, was an excellent lover, had the chemistry BUT he was full of it and wasn't 100%. Ishmael ain't Isaac. I want 100% what God has promised me. I am going to stop acting like Sarah and trying to rig it on my own and then get mad when it does not work!

Mr. Wrong #3
The Baby Pastor
SB:

(Living a double life and I found out on Facebook!!!)

Boy did I think this youngin" was all that. And we connected so. He reminded me of TW, but a younger, saved, God-loving TW. It was soooo refreshing to talk to a man about everything from music to scripture. He loved the Lord like me! He believed in giving like me. We were not just both Christian, we grew up the same denomination: COGIC. We seemingly held the same values about tithing, giving, praise, worship. We liked the same music. We laughed at each other's jokes. Wow! He is sooo mature for his age. OMG. And, I was not looking, just minding my business. I was not trying to make anything happen, it just happened. I had my doubts about someone so young and he lived in another state. I told myself I was being too rigid, just see what happens. If it meant to be it will be. Go with the flow.

SB and I met on a social networking site. We became friends in the Fall. Nothing big. He requested my friendship, I accepted. Just a hello from time to time. A "Have a blessed week" here and a "How was Church?" there and a "Check out my music." You know stuff like that. Somehow in May, our messaging grew. He would send a message, I would send a message, I would send a reply, he, in turn would send a reply.

He even left his number one time and said to call if I ever needed an ear or wanted to chat. It was May at this point. I was not planning on calling, but wrote back something to the effect of Ok, thanks, I will. One day he asked what our sermon at Church was about. I gave him some bullet points in a typed message. I asked what his sermon was about, and he asked if I would call because it was too much to type. That is how we started talking on the phone.

I had never done this before, but it seemed ok for some reason. We clicked instantly. We not only talked about the sermons, we talked about relationships, life, music, etc. He told me he had an album out. I told him I wanted to be supportive and I purchased his album off iTunes. (He is very talented by the way, and I really love some of his songs)

We talked again the next night. We talked about being in ministry, our families our Churches and the like. We had a nice conversation again. I asked him how old he was and he told me twenty-three. What! I told him how mature he seemed for his age and that he and I could only be brother and sister. He was simply too young.

He sent me a message a few days later saying: "I know you said we can only be brother and sister, but I feel a strong chemistry with you. Pray for me. LOL." I sent him a message back saying I felt it too, so he was going to have to pray for me as well. Let us just see what happens. We had planned to talk one night, but he did not call. No biggie I thought. He called me back a couple days after and left me the most beautiful message. He said he was sorry he did not call that night. He said he had spent three days in prayer, with no TV, limited cell phone and Internet use and was out witnessing. Now, what girl wouldn't understand that? Wow, I totally got it and I was very impressed.

We talked after that and continued to talk like every night. About a month later, my best friend came over one night and she told me not to be so available. She commented that he seems like a nice guy, but he is not making any efforts to get to your city to see you, so get your feelings in check and be careful. She was right. We would talk about visiting each other, but nothing really concrete. He had mentioned not being able to take time off work and how he had some time coming up in November. I told him by then, my new boyfriend and I would be showing him around. We laughed about that.

He had texted me that night my friend was over and I sent a short "K" response. He asked me if I was ok. I knew he meant because of my short response. I told him I was fine and that my friend was over and that we would talk later. He told me he felt put off. Huh? He later told me that it felt like I was not there for him or I was trying to brush him off somehow. But, he said he realized he had to get his feelings in check. He said I had not really done anything, it was him. It just let him know how he was truly feeling about me, and how we had gotten used to talking to and being there for one another. I told him I knew that short response probably prompted that. I knew instantly when I sent it and he responded back "Are you ok?" I knew he was feeling some sort of way. I had felt it too when he had done that to me with a short response. I even said something to the effect of: Oh, short, sweet and to the point huh?

We continued our phone conversations. We prayed for each other. We laughed. We shared intimate secrets and things about ourselves. Oh, how refreshing this was. Still trying to keep it in perspective. Still living my life doing me, but thinking about, hmmm what if? Don't be so rigid, you never know. You were not looking for

143

this. And, look how it has progressed from the Fall. He continued to tell me how he felt. We talked about his various speaking engagements, what scriptures he would use, etc. He was very excited when he was asked to give the sermon one Sunday. (I wonder now, if any of that was true) We talked about my daughter. He asked me how she would feel about us in a relationship. We talked about the age difference. Still no plans to actually meet. Just taking it all in.

I went on a job interview on my daughter's birthday and he was Johnny-on-the- spot with praying for me before I went and checking on me after to see how things went. I found out I did not get the job a couple days later and he again was calling to encourage me and check on me. He asked about my daughter's birthday and how it went. He seemed to be interested in my life. For a while in the beginning, it seem I was the one doing all the encouraging and inquiring, but he started to really want to know about my life, my child, my Church, my school, my plans, dreams, what I was doing, etc.

Shortly after that, I decided to take some time with God myself. It was late July at that point. A devotional I read and a sermon my bishop preached prompted me to take a week sabbatical with no cell phone or internet use and limited TV. When I told SB, he understood it right away. I knew he would because he had done the same thing a couple month's prior.

The week was awesome. I prayed for him everyday. I also prayed that this relationship be what God wanted it to be and nothing else. We had once talked about how even feeling connected to someone does not mean that they are the one. And how we sometimes get cloudy when we do meet someone we feel truly connected to. Ha!

What I found out after my mini sabbatical was shocking. He and I talked that Sunday. This was August 1st (You will see why I keep mentioning dates soon…very key.) He told me how much he missed talking to me. He said he wanted to call one night because he could not sleep. WOW. I joked and said, Oh I make you sleepy huh? I told myself, no, it is not that I make him sleepy but that I calm him. I listen and I pray for him and always seem to have just the right words to say. He told me that he felt my prayers. He had told me that before.

We talked about the music industry pulling on him and how it is hard to live for the Lord and be in the industry. We talked about some new possibilities he had and if he would go for it. He felt liked he was being pulled in two directions. He had been singing all his life and really wanted to make it in the industry, but God was calling him into ministry and lately he was being asked to speak not only at his own Church, but others as well.

I told him I would be praying for him. He told me this is why he really does not go on Facebook anymore because of the invites to perform, the lure of the world, people getting mad because he had to decline certain performances and blah, blah, blah. Hmmm, he had mentioned before that he really does not go on Facebook. I had told him that I am on it quite a bit, but I do like the site we met on a little more because of the groups and various forums. It never occurred to me to send him a friend's request on Facebook. I will have to do that I thought. No biggie. I had all ready checked out his My Space page and it was not really a personal page, but a page geared toward music and promoting his songs. I get that. Hey, it is free and lots of people promote that way.

145

We really did not talk the next couple days. He sent me a text bright and early that morning telling me he missed me, wanted to kiss me, blah, blah, blah. We texted a bit, but we did not talk. He called and told me that Wednesday, that it had been a little crazy and he was starting to learn a new job at work and blah, blah, blah. He said he had to teach Bible Study that night, but he would call me on his way home from work. I understood that. It does get busy some times and I knew he had a lot going on.

He had recently been put in charge of a big gala at his Church, he was speaking a lot and he was putting together a gospel concert for his union at work. He did call, but I was napping and missed it. He left me a message saying he is off work and about to go home, shower and study. He would call after we both got home from Bible Study and let me know how it went. Then he said I know you are praying for me, I am praying for you too. He sounded weird to me. He did earlier when we talked as well.

Well, something prompted me to request his friendship on Facebook that Wednesday. I put his name in and there he was in a photo with some chick on his profile page. WHAT!? It said in a relationship with and her name was there. It was in blue, so that means you can click it and go on her page. Girl, calm down. That could be his ex-girlfriend and didn't he say he had not been in a a relationship in a while? Well, I clicked it, it went to her page, and there they were again together. Different picture. She had "in a relationship with' and his name was there. She had the anniversary date as June 27. WHAT? Ok, girl that could mean that it will be a year on that date. And they broke up and neither of them has

146

been on here to change their profiles, etc. I really could not see anything else because both were set to private.

I did not hear from him Wednesday night, but I texted him the following on Thursday: Question: Are you still in a relationship with (I stated her name). You two photograph so nicely together. He did not respond back. Nothing. But do you know he accepted my friendship request? Yep. And boy did I find out plenty. He had let Facebook know that he had broken up with his ex-girlfriend in early June. Mind you, he told me all about what happened in late May and I thought it happened like earlier in the year. I did not know this was fresh. He got into a relationship with this one 20 days after that. Hence, the anniversary date. She came to visit him at the end of July. Right during the time I was on my sabbatical. She thanked him for showing her such a wonderful time while she was there and how thankful she was to have found him and how much she loved him. He wrote a status stating he could not wait to get some time off to go see his "wifey" in another city. WHAT?

I went to the Photo section, and there they were. The pictures were uploaded in late July and early August. They had posted pictures of them all hugged up together, uploaded from his phone no doubt. Did I mention he had told me once that he did not have a camera on his phone? He told me that his cousin helped him upload the pictures on the site we met on. He talked about not being tech savvy. Yeah right! People were commenting on how cute they looked together and how happy they were for him. Some commented that they thought this was rather soon. He commented back that he had no love for his past and how much he loved this one. WHAT? And of course his girlfriend commented on the pictures. Mushy, love you

147

baby kind of comments. There were plenty of comments on his profile page from her as well. WOW!

I was checking dates and messages on my phone wondering how in the world? There were also performances, events mentioned and photos that didn't jive with being at Church during certain times. There were dates that he commented on Facebook about his boo, that we had talked for hours. WOW! Why lie bruh? Now, he never promised me anything. We were not in a relationship, but he flat out lied. And, he never mentioned this to me. Why bother talking to me? Why bother getting to know me? Why tell me how you are falling "in like" with me? Why comment on my photos leading anyone who viewed them to believe that something was going on with us? And please tell me how you can use your love of the Lord, being called to ministry, etc. as an in with me? He told me about someone trying to set him up on a blind date. He told me about some women at Church that liked him and some lady from his job, but he NEVER told me about a relationship.

Perhaps, he used me to get over a rough patch. Perhaps talking to me and confiding in me was safe. Perhaps he did not know it was me he was accepting the friendship from. Or, perhaps accepting it was his way of coming clean. Perhaps, perhaps who knows. What I do know is what I've read is true. If a man truly wants to be with you, he will. He won't waste a whole bunch of time on the phone. I also know that God protects his children, answers prayer and reveals things in time. I know what God has for you is for you, but you must be patient and wait on Him. I know it was no coincidence that it came to me like it did. It's funny, during Bible Study that Wednesday night my bishop mentioned his city like two or three times. The message was about your connections

148

affecting your direction. Coincidence? I think not. Something went all through me that night and by the next day, it was all out in the open, I knew all I needed to know.

Getting to know someone is cool and much needed, but if there is to be any real relationship, a man would be trying to meet you in person, to know for sure. Now, I am not against meeting someone on a social networking site, but this experience for me, was definitely an eye opener!

Poem from the book,
**" *From the Womb to Wounded to Wonderful...*
*The Transformation***
by Lucky Caswell Harris.
Used with permission.

I Love too hard and I Love too strong.

Usually when I Love it turns out wrong.

I Love too long, I Love too deep

When I Love I Love for keeps.

I Love the idea of being in Love

I want that Love that is sent from above.

I Love to Love and be Love

But Love doesn't want the Love of my Love.

Resisting Red Flags

Every woman, man, and child is born with an internal radar system known as "intuition", "sixth sense", or "mother's wit". I was born with it too, but out of habit, conditioning, and desperation, I chose not to listen to my intuition. When I first met this man on my job in the summer of 1999, the inner alarm of my intuition was ringing loud and clear. There were multiple "red flags" warning me about this man's character and integrity during every stage of our relationship. The internal alarms kept ringing in the pit of my stomach as more "red flags" were revealed about this man. Instead of running for the hills and protecting myself from the hidden danger of this predator in disguise, I was very determined to prove that my intuition was wrong. Yet, my intuition knew that this man was a liar, a snake, a dog, a womanizer, a user, and an abuser.

"Red flags" are subtle, visible, and sometimes invisible clues in a relationship that warns you that something is "wrong" with the person you are dating. The devil always shows his face before he is about to attack. All the "red flags" indicated that I was dealing with a sociopath and a very dangerous predator. I had dreams and visions of this man being a predator. I even came across books and other sources of information that alerted me that I was dating a predator. All this information fell into my lap without any effort on my part. God was trying to get my attention through my intuition, dreams, visions, friends, family, and various media. Yet, I was on a mission to prove that this man was a good man. I walked right into this man's trap with my eyes wide open and purposely closed the door to God's warnings of impending danger. Since I made a conscious choice to ignore those "red flags", I became the perfect victim in an abusive relationship that consumed my life for ten years. Welcome to the world of "Resisting Red Flags". Welcome to a life filled with abuse, betrayal, mind games, lies, manipulations, heavy financial and personal losses, insanity, drama, trauma, and sexual assault, as the cycle of abuse repeats itself over, and over, and over again. Welcome to the habit of volunteering for the role of being the "Perfect Victim" for the "Perfect Power Pimping Predator". This man was not the first predator to invade my life. I had a hopeless addiction to sex, abusive men, and predators.

Many years ago, around the age of five, I was molested by a close friend of the family. This man was so sick and so twisted that he introduced me to sexual acts that would blow a grown woman's mind. Because, I was a child experiencing the trauma of abuse, I became fragmented in my mind and in my soul. Every time, this man molested me and raped me, I learned to escape my body and enter the realm of the "out-of-body" experiences. My tiny spirit would float to the ceiling and watch the horror of my own abuse from above. I would no longer be present within myself. When the abuse was over, I would rejoin my body and act as if nothing happened. As far as I was concern, the whole thing was just a bad dream and it really did not exist.

Unfortunately, that experience set me up to become the Perfect Victim for the Predators of this world. Since my spirit was detached from my body during most of my waking moments, it was very easy for me to "resist red flags". I ignored "red flags". I did not pay attention to them. I was oblivious to them. The word danger had no meaning to me. I would walk into dangerous situations with my eyes wide open. I would fall into the arms of predators without giving it a second thought. Throughout my life, I was raped, abused, misused, and treated like a puppet on a string, all in the name of love. I did not know how to be in a healthy, loving, wholesome relationship with a normal man, but I did know how to be the perfect victim in an abusive relationship with a predator.

My self-protection system was damaged as a result of my childhood rape experiences. My parents did not protect me from my molester because they did not believe me when I tried to tell them what was happening to me. Since they did not protect me, it just made it seem okay to my little girl's mind, for predators to seek me out and devour me without resistance on my part. I became a walking feast for predators that crossed my path. They were my boyfriends, lovers, dates, casual acquaintances, and so called friends. I had no boundaries when it came to men. I was a "space cadet" with a beautiful face and a sexy body. The word "no" was not a part of my vocabulary. I did not feel like I had the right to protect my body. I was conditioned to believe from my abuse experiences that my body belonged to anybody who wanted it. I was conditioned to believe that sex meant love. I taught myself to believe that I was molested because it was my destiny to become a sex object for men to play with, exploit, and abuse.

When I became tired of being a victim, I decided to become a predator and I called myself the "Black Widow". Black Widow spiders mate and then kill their mates. In my case, I seduced men and then broke their hearts. I flipped the script and become the bold, sexy, hot mama, who controlled the sexual encounters with men. I used men for sex and threw them away like trash after I was done with them. I became very promiscuous and had various one night stand encounters with total strangers whom I felt I could manipulate and control. I felt very powerful and high from that dangerous and reckless lifestyle. However, after each sexual conquest, I would fall into a deep depression and look for another man to give me that power fix again. That lifestyle eventually led to a nervous breakdown. I was giving up my soul and peace of mind to have a little bit of power in my life. I allowed evil to rule me and I descended into my own personal hell of darkness. I did not realize that what I needed was healing from my abusive experience. God saved me from hell when he intervened and stopped me from having what would have been my fourth abortion.

I spent my entire adult life with a broken self-protection system, damaged boundaries, no sense of self, a fragmented mind, heart, soul, and spirit, and an addiction to sex and abusive men. After my nervous breakdown, I took a five-year hiatus from sex. I was celibate. I needed to cleanse my soul from all those soul-ties that were created from my acting out days. I spent my 20s being a dog and/or a victim. I spent my 30s recovering from my 20s. I joined 12 step programs for sex and love addicts. I went into therapy to deal with my addiction. When I finally hit 40 years old, I thought I was ready to fall in love and to have a legitimate relationship with a good man. What I failed to realized was that I still had a lot of healing to do in my soul before I was ready to be in a healthy relationship. Because I was still damaged and wounded from my childhood, my predator radar was still operating in my psyche. I was still attracted to predators. I was still addicted to predators. Predators were still attracted to me. This is where my story begins with my "Resistance to Red Flags".

In spite of everything God tried to do to steer me away from another dangerous and abusive predator, I resisted the red flags that were screaming in my face. The

154

man I fell in love in the summer of 1999, was a liar, a snake, a dog, a womanizer, a user, and an abuser. He was as sick and twisted as they could come. I was very sick and twisted for allowing myself to become involved with him. When we first met, everything within my spirit was screaming, "Run, run, run!" Yet, everything in my addictive mind was screaming , "Yes, yes, yes!" I said "yes" to his lies. I said "yes" to his mind games and manipulations. I said "yes" to drinking hard liquor against my will. I said "yes" to his obvious womanizing lifestyle. I even said "yes" when he convinced me that I was the one who gave him the same STD three years in a row during the month of May. Even though I knew that he was the only man I was sleeping with…I still said "yes" to his accusations of infidelity. I said "yes" to his broken promises. I said "yes" when he was stingy with his money yet always finding ways to get me to spend my money on him. I said "yes" when I caught him cheating red handed. I said "yes" when he isolated me from my family and friends. I said "yes" to acts of sex that degraded my dignity as a woman. I said "yes" to sexual behaviors that went against my self-worth as a woman. I said "yes" when he forced me to turn down a scholarship to attend graduate school to get my master's degree for free. He promised to pay for schooling later but again more broken promises. I said "yes" when I volunteered for the role of being his perfect sex toy and victim. I was his perfect little puppet on a string.

Throughout the ten years of abuse, trauma, drama, mind games, manipulations, lies, broken promises, betrayal with other women behind my back, I felt lost inside my mind, spirit, heart and soul. I was completely detached from myself and from the reality of my nightmare. I prayed so hard for deliverance. I felt so fragmented within myself. I stayed with him because on the surface, he looked like a good catch. It was good for my image and self-esteem to be with him. He was a professional with a college degree, a good income, property, and cars. He had various hustles to produce multiple incomes. I stayed with him because he said he loved me and that he would never cheat on me even though in my spirit I knew that I was not the only woman in his life. I stayed with him because he had a sexy muscular body and a well-endowed penis for a man his age even though the sex was very painful. I stayed with him because I was afraid of being alone. I stayed with him for the rare good times that did take place in between episodes of abuse and infidelity. I stayed with him because I thought he was my last chance for happiness, love, and marriage. I stayed with him because I believed that no one else would want me if I broke up with him because of my older age. I stayed for his promises of a better life. I stayed with him because I could not love myself enough to walk away. I allowed that man to control my destiny and my identity and my dreams.

As I stayed and prayed for deliverance, I started going back to 12 step meetings. I started going back to therapy. I went back to school and pursued my own interests. I started reading a lot of self-help books to help me understand my condition as a woman who is addicted to abusive men and sex. I started working on my spiritual walk with God. I started keeping a journal throughout the entire relationship. The journal was a lifesaver. The journal kept me connected with reality in case I would slip into denial about being with a predator and an abuser. I stopped having sex with him. I stopped spending my weekends with him. I stopped buying into his mind games. I stopped fighting him so there was no more drama for him to control me with. I stopped letting him have space in my head. I started thinking for myself. I started believing in my self and my self-worth. I started trusting my perceptions and my

156

intuition about his lies and his secret double life with other women. Through it all, I started to love myself by the grace and love of God.

As I prayed my way into wholeness, God kept whispering to my spirit that he was slowly knitting my soul back together again, so that when I became whole, I would have the courage and the strength to walk away and to never look back. I hooked up with my abusive predator on July 20, 1999. I finally walked out of his life forever on June 26, 2009. Ten years of hell finally came to an end.

Because I am a survivor of childhood sexual abuse, I have accepted the fact that I will always be vulnerable to predators like an alcoholic is vulnerable to alcohol. I practice self-awareness and acceptance of my emotional condition as a survivor of abuse. I understand that predators are broken people. They look for women like me to manipulate, control, abuse, use, and exploit. Victims like me, are broken people also. It was our condition of brokenness that drew us to each other. Predators and victims are broken people in need of love, grace, and forgiveness from God to heal their brokenness.

I am grateful for the lessons I've gained from this last relationship. I am grateful that I have been able to understand and to learn how my own diseased thinking would allow me to resist red flags and to seek out predators. I have a greater understanding of my sick and twisted need to be with a predator. It is what I have become comfortable with as a result of my abuse. Just because being abused feels comfortable and natural to me doesn't mean that I have to live that way for the rest of my life. I deserve more. I deserve better. Loving and trusting God is what is best for my life.

157

As a result of this experience I have learned the following valuable lessons on listening to red flags, living, and loving myself:

R = **Resist evil**.   My self-protection skills are working now. I know that I have a right to resist evil and to protect myself from predators in spite of what happened to me as a child.

E = **Endure trials**. It was very difficult for me to break my addiction to my predator. Yet, I hung in there like a champ. I prayed. I attended meetings. I went to therapy. I did an inventory of myself. I did affirmations. I praised God. I went to Church. I read the Bible. I endured the pain of withdrawal. I endured the emptiness of being alone with myself. Yet God is so good. God filled up my soul with his light and love. Now my cup runneth over.

D = **Delay gratification.** It was my hunger for love and my desperation to be in a relationship that made me very vulnerable to this predator. Predators seek out women who are lonely, desperate, empty, and emotionally needy. I was so needy when I met this man, that it was very easy for him to get over on me with lies, broken promises, and mind games. If I were in my right mind when I met him, I would have immediately cut him off at the sign of the very first red flag. Don't let a man rush you into the bedroom or rush you into a commitment before you get a chance to find out his true character. Just wait, watch, and win the dating game.

F = **Faith conquers Fear**; Forgiveness conquers Frustration. My faith in God conquered my fears of leaving and my fears of being alone. Today I am single. I am content. I am at peace with myself. My age is no longer an issue. I believe that love can be found at any stage of an adult woman's life. Having forgiveness towards the predators and abusers of my past relieves me of experiencing the frustration of having regrets or seeking revenge. I plead the blood of Jesus over all sins I committed against others as well as sins committed against me.

L = **Live, love, and laugh**. In my recovery, I strive to live in the present, love from the abundance of Christ's love for us, and laugh for the sheer joy of being free and alive in Christ.

A = **Acceptance.** I practice the art of having acceptance. In having acceptance for the things I cannot change, God has given me the courage to change the things I can and the wisdom to know the difference.

G = **Grace of God.** I am very thankful to experience the Grace of God in my life. I was dealing with a predator who was a cold-hearted sociopath. A sociopath is a person who has no conscious at all. A sociopath has no normal or real human emotions. He will use and abuse people just for the sheer delight of it. My predator was a sociopath. It is by the grace of God that I was able to escape with my life intact. God still had a hold on a piece of my mind and set me free. I thank God everyday for another day of peace and freedom away from that dangerous, cruel, and evil man.

S = **Seek Ye First the Kingdom of God.** I put God first in my life. Putting God first in my life has opened the door for a deep healing and cleansing of my wounded soul. I have tasted the Lord and he is sooooo good to me!!! In Jesus, name I pray Amen.

The combined letters above spell the word "RED FLAGS". Never again will I ignore my intuition, which is the voice of God speaking to my spirit. Never again, will I ignore the subtle signals of red flags alerting me to danger in a relationship. I thank God everyday, for teaching me how to listen and respect the messages of " red flags" in an encounter with a man. Women of the world, please listen to your intuition when you are dating a new man. Please pay close attention to the "red flags" that may pop up during your courtship. When those "red flags" pop up....RUN....RUN....RUN....AND DON'T LOOK BACK!!!! Please trust your intuition. God gave us intuition for a reason. The life you are protecting and saving could be your very own life.

Beat Down

I met a man about 19 or so years ago. We had a casual relationship, which simply means we saw each other and spent time together. He was what I call a "Wanderer" and a "Loner", never staying still, always in the streets, but he had many friends and he would visit us often.

I was raising my children, so it was the perfect relationship for me. He was kind and smart. He listened and shared and he was very handsome. He was eighteen and I was twenty-five. Yes, after having my children, all I wanted was a younger man. Having been on his own since he was thirteen, he was strong, self-sufficient and well respected in the streets.

Three years after I met him, a couple of males from our neighborhood (losers) that we knew, stomped him out leaving him for dead. I never knew what happened to him since he was not connected to anyone, not even his parents.

Maybe five years later, I got word that he was in fact still alive, but I could not find him and I had never stopped wanting to find him. Recently, I was going to attend a workshop and I saw his name under the attending list, my heart started racing and I contacted the person in charge. Finally, after sixteen years, I found him. I sent him a message to which he responded. Later, I found out it was the "person that housed him" that responded, not him. He asked to see me and we began to talk, he soon revealed that he did not remember me at all. I realized that he was surrounded by people who did not know him before his "accident", as he calls it. Just three years before I found him, he was just learning how to walk and talk against all odds.

My friend had sustained life long injuries as a result of HIS "beat down". His pelvis was displaced so his equilibrium is off center and he can no longer straighten up. His legs were reconstructed so many times he has minimal to no control over them and he has minimal use of his hands. He has to take several medications because he now suffers from a bad heart, and until maybe a year ago, seizures were threatening his life. He has suffered from brain damage, which has affected his memory. He can only remember the friends he had starting from age 2, which are my dear friends as well. The person that housed him was a health care provider so he only qualified for twelve hours per day of care, which was dangerous because after a certain hour he is left alone, because she can no longer go up and down steps.

I started spending time with him and we were so happy because I was growing spiritually and his memory was brand new. We decided that we would like to build a more meaningful relationship. We would talk for hours and we spent time together watching movies he selected. He would invite me to his Church. We would drive around, eat together, go to the park, and just enjoy each other. Eventually it was requested that I spend more time around as I call her the "wicked witch", the lady that had housed him under the assumption that he would be of a vegetative state for the rest of his life. At the time I was grateful for such a safe place to heal his body when he had no one else. Keep in mind, no one had taken up any time with him. He stayed in the basement and was miserable with no personal contacts, just nurses, doctors, home health aids.

I learned about how his meds were administered and he started spending the night. We were forming a wonderful give and take relationship, because as in the

162

past, he was an extremely caring man. He was wise and sharing and he got along with my family very well. In spite of the fact that he could barely keep his balance, he loved to clean and rearrange things. He loved to buy foods that were healthy yet tasted good. He was interested in how my world operated and became apart of it, as I did the same with him, going to doctor appointments, becoming familiar with the people that he had been around for five years because he was initially going to be in a facility for the remainder of his life. Eventually talk of staying with me more and building toward a lifelong relationship was discussed on his part given the tireless love I gave him. You see it was like I was his first girlfriend, and I certainly had been the first in sixteen years.

Then all hell broke loose. Suddenly the person that housed him began getting involved because he wanted to live with me. You see, by day I showed him love and by night he shared it with the person that housed him and she twisted it. All the trust, the love, the caring, the long agonizing talks (because of the extremely small hole in his throat that caused him to have to learn how to say words again), and the genuine affection that my family and I shared with him were all made dirty and tainted in his mind.

Now the fact that we watched TV together in his space meant I was spying on him. Although when we went out to eat I always paid in contrast to his dollar store trips that he wanted to take me on that never happened, it was said I might use him. The reaction that I would convey in regard to the personal care assistants disrespecting me was turned around and painted as just a jealous act on my part. For what reason would a woman like myself want to be involved with a man with such needs other than out of love? The concern to be involved with his health care,

163

which to me was a necessity given our goal to spend a future together, and the desire that we had for each other physically was said to be a way for me to manipulate him. In the beginning he thought that I was sexy. Now he said that I was slutty, trampy and ungodly. My hair, which was beautiful and different to him before, now indicated that I was controlling and wanted to be a man.

The trips to the park were no longer pleasurable, but viewed as manipulation time. The fact that I took time to help him pronounce words, at his request, of course, was said to be done because I wanted to take his manhood away. Before, God was a strong bond that we shared; now I was a devil worshiper. My family ties that he loved the interaction with, now needed to be adjusted all together. I did not love them as he would have. I would be loved by day and hated by night. Eventually the emotional roller coaster ride was over for me. I had spoken with the one person that did care about him, while I continued to pray exhaustively. I had convinced myself that since he spoke of God so frequently he knew Him. Yet in his eyes, as he told me one day he was God and I was to worship him. When I gathered all my pieces, and took my leave I was threatened, harassed, belittled, and told that I was trying to manipulate him through sex.

SEX! If you don't know, a man with these circumstances can only have an effective sex life in his MIND!!!! I thank God that I was able to get out and remain faithful to Him. However to this day, the threats that I have received to kick doors in, break windows out, slap me, and kick my a** continue. I am still loved and hated by the same man. Three weeks of moving forward and five weeks of torment. It is now five months later and I don't miss a day of text messages and voice mails all day. In the rare event that I answer, I am informed that I must stop treating him like a punk. He made a mistake and is sorry and wants another chance. However, by the end of the conversation I am the lowest form of a human being on earth.

That being said, my message to women is…if you are being subjected to this emotional abuse… Do Not Stay. Keep in mind that there is more than one form of abuse: mental, physical, emotional and financial. Get out! This is nothing new and if he says he will change, you pray for him but do not allow him to drag you down in the process. No matter what a man's circumstances abuse is abuse.

To God be the glory for the things He has done. Psalms 23

Abuse is not a reflection on you…unless you stay.

Kimberly Whitmore

Heaven Sent

Mr. Wrong

The father of my kids is definitely a "Mr. Wrong". At the time I met him, I thought I was in love and ready to have his children. I did. We never got married. He ended up in prison leaving me alone with one child. I ended up on drugs. When he came out of prison, I ended up having another child with this same man.

He was not there for me for either one of the children's births. I had to endure childbirth alone. My children's father eventually ended up with an 85-year prison sentence. I turned to drugs and was in and out of jail, etc.

The kids were with their grandparents. I was in no position to raise them by myself with my addictions. So many things were going on all at the same time. We did not have GOD in our lives.

Mr. Right

After years of this viscous cycle, I finally truly found God and turned my life around. I have been clean and sober for five years now and could not have done it without God in my life. Every year is a milestone in my life, in 2006 I was released from Prison, 2007 I got my son back, 2008 I got my daughter back, 2009 I bought my house, in 2010 I stopped smoking cigarettes after twenty years and also reunited with Mr. Right. In 2011 we plan on marrying.

He found me after 20 years....we went out back then but went our separate ways. Every since then, he has not stopped looking for me. Now that he has found me, he refuses to lose me again.

This is the man of my dreams, I prayed and prayed that God would just drop someone down from Heaven and land in my lap....and that's what happened.

After a series of bad relationships and hardships, finally in God's time, we are together. God knew that finally, we were both ready. We are both in our 40's and have never been married. This was worth the wait. He is a Godly man and wants to set a good example and wants us to be married before we live together, etc. It impressed me that he even blessed the food on our first date.

Together, we have a lot to be thankful for. We are grateful to God, for what we both know in our hearts, is a match made in heaven.

The Suit Doesn't Make the Man

He came into my life, handsome, advanced degrees and very well dressed. I had known this man since the playground days. As we grew older entering high school, I can recall him asking me out on dates and me always refusing to give him the time of day. Although he was a great swimmer, played tennis and had a musical gift, back then if you didn't have ties with the popular kids, I didn't have time for you. We all know the same story just different times. Well upon graduating from high school we lost connection, which for me was not the worst thing. I always felt that he was just a little too interested in me. Even still, it was still nice for someone to shower so much attention on me.

We went on with our lives, I got married and he did the same. We were each having children and enjoying life. As our lives changed, we each found ourselves no longer in our marriages. I believe that it is important to point out that during my life, from college, to marriage, to a child this man had secretly kept tabs on me. I was never aware of this until after he and I started to date. This was the first clue that I missed. The internet was not my friend, although I had not talked to this man for close to twenty years, it was as if he recounted that time with precision. I got a call from my mother telling me that I got a call from an old friend from school and that he wanted to connect with me; second clue. How did he get my parents unlisted number? I missed that clue as well.

Since I was going through a divorce, I welcomed the opportunity to talk to someone from my past that appeared to be doing great. We had so much to catch up on, so I dialed the number with a mixture of excitement and numbness. As one hour turned to two, to four and then to six on the phone, I wondered why we had not dated in the past. I would soon find out.

We planned to see each other. He planned to come to Cleveland and we would go out to dinner. He showed up well dressed, smelling good and sounding good, but the suit don't make the man. We had a great dinner and wonderful conversation. (Because let him tell it, it was because of his advanced degrees that he was able to talk so knowledgeable on so many topics. Are you serious? That sounds a little narcissistic but what do I know, I only have a degree in Psychology.)

As the relationship grew, I became swept off of my feet. I allowed this man to move into my home before my divorce was even final. What was I thinking? When he moved in, his bags were not even unpacked good before he flipped the script. The man who I thought I knew started to show his controlling side, his condescending ways and then came the abuse. He dressed the abuse in such a way that I thought it was me. I started to question myself, wondered how this could be happening; and that is just what he wanted. I learned that the signs of an abusive man could range from emotional, verbal, and physical. He had all the combinations. I understood that the signs of an abusive man can usually be found out after a few dates, if only I had paid attention, asked questions and did some investigating into his past.

His passion for success allowed him to create a recruiting firm with several locations. As he and his company grew, he began receiving invitations for speaking engagements. His reputation and knowledge on workplace diversity issues became well known, but then his house of cards began to crumble. In public, we were perfect, smiling and shaking hands. The couple that reconnected from early childhood was the story, "how sweet" I can recall people

169

saying. Then it started, the first abuse was the combination of control games mixed in with jealousy. He became so skilled at it, it was hard to pinpoint. I remember him telling me that since I did not care for him that he wanted to end his life. He went downstairs, returned saying that he had drank some bleach, and that he was going to walk to his grandmother's gravesite to die. Shocked, I called his mother in hopes of getting some support, I would later find out that this behavior was the norm for her son. This man would tell me that he loved me and that he would change, in order for me to stay. Empty promises became the norm. Why didn't I pay attention to his actions and not merely his words? I forgot the old saying that says, "Actions, speak louder than words."

The second act of abuse came while I was driving. I decided that I no longer wanted to attend a particular event. Hot coffee was knocked out of my hand and wasted all over me and the interior of my car. As the actions began to escalate, the danger began to increase to the point I remember being held against my will after being knocked down some stairs.

That night I began to put together my plan...I got up early packed a bag and left my home. I called a friend of his and spoke to both he and his wife, and explained the situation to him. My mouth hit the floor when he said, "He is doing it again...I thought he got help."

By this point, I was long gone from the house and once my boyfriend knew that I spoke with his friend he started to call my phone, which seemed like every few minutes. He cried, begged, and said that he was sorry for all that he had done. He wanted me to come and talk to him. I was a little stronger and better able to say no. After he left my home that night, relief allowed me to sleep.

As the days turned into weeks, I realized that he was not going to let me go that easy. The phone calls continued, then came a dozen roses sent to my home daily. I tried to rebuild my life for my daughter and me. As I moved away from that part of my life, I started to date a great guy and we later married. The story does not end there because my husband became a victim of this man's sick obsession. Even though years have passed, I am still haunted by the pain. I am constantly reminded that the suit does not make the man.

It is important to know some key things about abusive relationships. Abusive relationships are never abusive in the beginning, if they were, women would dump the abusive man immediately in search of a good man. According to the American Psychological Association Force on Violence and Family, over 4 million American women experience a serious assault by a partner each year.

Abusive behavior touches all ranges of society. If your partner exhibits one or more of these signs, it may be time to reevaluate your relationship and seek help or get out.

1. **Jealousy & Possessiveness** – Becomes jealous over your family, friends, and co-workers. Tries to isolate you. Views his woman and children as his property instead of as unique individuals. Accuses you of cheating or flirting with other men without cause. Always asks where you have been and with whom in an accusatory manner.

2. **Control** – He is overly demanding of your time and must be the center of your attention. He controls finances, the car, and the activities you partake in. Becomes angry if woman begins showing signs of independence or strength.

3. **Superiority** – He is always right, has to win or be in charge. He always justifies his actions so he can be "right" by blaming you or others. A verbally abusive man will talk down to you or call you names in order to make him feel better. The goal of an abusive man is to make you feel weak so they can feel powerful. Abusers are frequently insecure and this power makes them feel better about themselves.

4. **Manipulates** – Tells you that you are crazy or stupid so the blame is turned on you. Tries to make you think that it is your fault he is abusive. Says he cannot help being abusive so you feel sorry for him and you keep trying to "help" him. He tells others that you are unstable.

5. **Mood Swings** – His mood switches from aggressive and abusive to apologetic and loving after the abuse has occurred.

6. **Actions don't match words** – He breaks promises, says he loves you and then abuses you.

7. **Punishes you** – An emotionally abusive man may withhold sex, emotional intimacy, or plays the "silent game" as punishment when he doesn't get his way. He verbally abuses you by frequently criticizing you.

8. **Unwilling to seek help** – An abusive man does not think that there is anything wrong with him so why should he seek help? Does not acknowledge his faults or blames it on his childhood or outside circumstances.

9. **Disrespects women** – Shows no respect towards his mother, sisters, or any of the women in his life. Thinks women are stupid and worthless.

The Bureau of Justice Statistics states that on the average, more than three women are murdered by their husbands or boyfriends every day. So please be careful. If your partner is not willing to seek help for his abusive behavior, your only option is to leave.

Don't Eat the Rice

I was never a wild person, foolish...yes. I got married to my first boyfriend, while yet a teenager. After a tumultuous 12-year marriage and four children later, I found myself a young divorcee.

Even though the first marriage was a disaster, I thanked God for my children and knew that He was going to send me the real "Mr. Right" someday.

Twelve years and a few "You Ain't the Ones" and a couple of "You're Definitely Not the Ones", I met the man of my dreams. He was a new client and he wanted me to manage the financial affairs of his business. With four teens at home, I needed all of the money I could get. This handsome fellow worked with my father, and in my mind had my father's seal of approval.

I later found out that this fellow had a rather wild past but was finally completing a turn around. My father had been instrumental in pleading his case at the job, assuring people that he was a sincere, dedicated and truly changed young man. However, Bruce informed me that it was my grandfather, years earlier as a young child that had taught him and other young boys on the block to "shoot crap, roll blunts and chase women." (I never knew he even knew my grandfather!)

Bruce had recently accepted his calling into the ministry. His business was very successful and he had a good job. He was raising his two children on his own and was an excellent father. He made his daughters feel like princesses. Everything they wanted he made sure it was provided, including brand new sports cars.

174

I was introduced to them as the accountant. They knew my children from school. It all seemed perfect. In the back of my mind, we were all preparing to become the new and improved Brady Bunch.

Bruce soon grew to trust me and depend on me outside of the business context. He put my name on his bank accounts, I was at his beck and call. He was a very studious and dedicated man. He was working full-time, in Theology school full time, raising his daughters, running his business and very active in his Church. He really needed my help and I was more than willing to give it. Even though it put me behind on my assignments, I loved typing his sermons.

We were both saved and loved the Lord with all of our hearts. With all of the duties he had entrusted me with, I felt that this Man of God was testing me to see if I would make a good First Lady. I was determined to pass the test. I knew in my mind he was my "Mr. Right".

He purchased a beautiful new home. He allowed me to pick the furniture. He sent me to pay for the furniture, wait on the delivery people and give them directions where to place it. In my heart, I kept thanking God for this handsome man and this beautiful house and the new life I knew God was preparing me for.

He worked nights, near my house and would often call me at 11:00 p.m. and ask me to bring him $40.00 of his money and to get $20.00 for myself. As a single mom, trying to maintain my own home, I always welcomed extra money. He paid me for my accounting services, but he also allowed me to use any of his money, as long as I put it back before the bills were due. It made me feel special. He never kept money on him. I figured it was his way of making sure we saw each other often.   I did not mind, because we talked on the phone two or three times a day, and I had to meet him several times a week to give him money…his own money. He often wanted me to bring his favorite meal, Chinese rice. Along with all the other good qualities, Bruce took excellent care of his health. Rice was one of his favorite foods, any style, and any kind.

One day, about a year into our friendship, Bruce called me for an emergency meeting. As we sat in his beautiful new truck, he explained to me that some things he had done in his past were finally catching up with him. Even though he has been clean for five or six years, he used to be a mess. After a huge grand jury sweep, his past had caught up with him. Now as a minister of the Gospel, he could not lie and was willing to face his punishment. Because he had made such a tremendous turn around, the authorities allowed him to keep his job and report to jail nights and weekends.

He gave me orders that while he was in jail, to continue to run his business, watch his house and give his daughters their weekly allowance. They were capable of taking care of themselves and buying their own food. I just needed to go to his account and give them the money when needed.

He continued to tell me that I was the only one he could trust, and that he thanked God for me.

The period of time went so fast. I continued to handle his business – even more than I handled my own.

He continued in school. I loved typing and editing his sermons. We would stay up on the phone late into the midnight hours. He taught me how to break down the

176

Bible…exegete it. He loved learning Hebrew and Greek. Any question I had, I would call Bruce. I loved how he would tell me the history of the era first, then the customs, then explain the passage I had in question. He enjoyed explaining it as much as I enjoyed learning it.

In my mind it was all perfect. Bruce was a dedicated Man of God, loving father, excellent provider. In my mind, he was capable of being my spiritual leader and covering I so needed and desired. We would live the good life in his mini-mansion. I would continue to run his business, take care of his children, (who were pretty self-sufficient), help him run his Church, and one day get the love and affection I so yearned from a man.

Once Bruce got through with his jail time, he was even more involved with the Lord. He and I distanced ourselves, physically, not wanting the temptation of displeasing the Lord. He wanted to do right and be right. I was grateful. I loved the Lord and did not like failing Him in anyway, not even five minutes.

Soon weeks would pass, then months. Three months after we had last spoken, I got a call from Bruce. In my mind, I thought he was taking time to readjust with his children after the jail sentence. I got excited when the phone rang and I saw that he was calling me. He was so excited. He had an announcement. Bruce was getting married. He had found a simple country girl, suited just for him. He said that I would never be pleased with him as I yearned to travel and see the world, while he was just a country boy and loved to stay around the house. He said that I was used to the finer things of life, with my downtown office, TV show, bank presidency, board positions and after all he was just a simple man.

177

My heart sunk. I didn't know what to think. He continued on to say that as a "dear friend" to he and his family, he would be honored if I attended the wedding.

The bride looked absolutely stunning as she walked in with the veil over her face. As I eagerly awaited the removal of the veil to see who replaced me, my mouth fell to my chest. The bride was the spitting image of me! It was incredible. A visual image of me, only twenty pounds lighter (I knew I should have lost the weight!) Usually it is hard for a person to see the resemblance of someone who looks like them, but in this case, it was unmistakable. After the beautiful ceremony, I fought back the tears through the vows.

After the vows, an announcement was made," Don't throw the rice." They explained that the birds eat it and it fills their bellies and swells, they get sick or worse, they die. They announced that there was birdseed available to toss at the Bride and Groom instead. I had never heard of this. For all my years, even in the movies I always saw them throwing rice at weddings. I thought to myself, my, how things change.

It was time for the Bride and Groom to walk down the isle, out into their promising future together. I harbored no ill feelings towards him. He was still "Mr. Right", but the reality of the matter was that I was not his choice for "Mrs. Right". The Bride looked beautiful, like a beautiful exotic bird...white, pure, fluffy, carefree and rested.

Aisle by aisle the guests walked down and out of the Church. When the ushers indicated that it was time for my row to walk out, I walked down that same isle...alone. As I walked out, I felt like a bird too... a street pigeon-dull, tired, and worn out...with a belly full of rice.

For years, I had eaten the rice. Rice...small... insignificant by itself, usually requiring something more substantial to dress it up. Rice...the tiny little seemingly insignificant "white lies". In my mind he was saying, "I never said we would get married...I just had you pick the furniture, handle the money, pay the bills, take care of the kids, drive the cars, type the sermons and run the Church."

Truth be told, he didn't tell me he was testing me for the First Lady position. I was so eager to have the perfect man, house, and picket fence, I cooked the rice myself, telling myself the little, tiny white lies and dressing them up to my liking.

Looking back, I now see that any little thing he did, I analyzed it, mulled it over and in any way, shape or form made it fit my version of "our" story.

As I prepared to leave the Church grounds, his oldest daughter came running up to me and hugged me, so sincerely. One of the tears I had fought back during the ceremony escaped through the corner of my eye as our eyes met and locked for a second or two. I felt her heart racing as we embraced. I heard her heart speak..."I thought it would be you." Fighting desperately to hold back the second tear, knowing that it would cause a flood of tears if I let it out, my heart spoke back to hers... "Me too."

The worst lies are the ones we tell ourselves.

A poem by Jacqueline Gillon
Used with permission
J E G Lyrical Princess 08/08/09

TRUE STORY

Hometown Honey
You're fantasy's best.
No less than what I had dreamed of
Always out of reach.
Even as children my heart would beat so
Like a drum
Hoping you would come down the street
On your bike
Or at least to deliver our newspaper.
40 years past grown now
And miles separate us.
But cell phone and text
E-mail and air travel
We are sharing
Life in the third gear.
How about a try now
Beyond one day stand land
I want a lifetime commitment man.
From my friend for life
Who else could I trust
Our Moms and Dads
Old confidantes
Lives changing as they age.
My Dad already gone away
Who else could I trust?
But underneath our connection
Lies your real intentions
A slight omission of a wife tucked away

In another State.
They had to appear one day
Sad day at your Mother's home going.
I'm going crazy with the news
How carefully God has forced deceit's hand
To tell the truth
Of having your cake and eating it too!

Is He the One or Shall I Look For Another?

"Is he the one or shall I look for another?" This seemed to be my college mantra. How many times did I think "he" is the one? Let me count the times…let me see…we can start with college. There were a couple of times in high school but by college, I really thought I knew what love was. In college, I think I deceived myself about three times. We will call my freshman year man, "Chicago…Windy City Blessings". He had a voice and eyes that literally caused every part of me to melt. He was highly intellectual, a man's man and a brotha thru and thru…but, he was not the one.

Then there was my "Sophomore S"more" …chocolate for days with the most perfect white teeth. My junior year was "crazy"…crazy. By my senior year, I started to wonder, "Where is he?" I had not yet figured out the issue may not be them, but me. But, what was my issue? After college, like a lot of women, career, marriage and children were my hope, a hope that eluded me. My first out of college real love was a man about ten years older than me who presented such an illusion of perfection. He was everything I thought my list called for. (Those lists have gotten a lot of sistahs in trouble; particularly when they were created out of our fleshly, fairy tale, fraudulent selves.) He was well spoken, well groomed and well tailored. He was a local media personality, who commanded a room. He had the look of stability, He had beautiful brown chocolate skin. He was a great communicator, health conscious, a satisfying and pleasing lover and a suitable companion. For almost two years, if in this city during the 90"s there was a power couple, it would have been us.

He was the first man I travelled with and introduced to my family as my "man". He was the first man I had "a stars and stripes fireworks" climax with, (an experience shared about one or two weeks prior to the relationship falling apart). Whatever I desired, he made sure it was taken care of. If he could not be there or do it – he made sure it got done. A real man, right? After an amazing Valentine's Day weekend, a year and a half in…totally "in love"…having asked Brian McKnight to sing at our wedding (really),..surely this was it…right?

It was a Saturday, I cannot remember if it was late afternoon or evening. I do remember walking out to the pond happy and excited. I think I thought, "This is the day, he is going to ask me to marry to him."

There he was sitting on the bench. As I approached, I knew something was wrong by the look on his face. He had his head down. (How did I see his face? I guess I felt it.) In that very moment my stomach sank – a quick dive. Suddenly, a confession of necessity brought our relationship to an abrupt halt…he was about to be a daddy again. I cannot tell you what he said – I literally lost my ability to hear. The ex-girlfriend I always had suspicions of, was pregnant and due any day.

It was a confession of necessity because it was not out of love or respect that he told me. It was out of fear and the reality that he could hide it no longer. During the nine months of an eighteen-month relationship he was living and we were representing a lie. I think that was the biggest hurt. For most women, I believe the deception is the biggest pain. Ok, they have sex with another woman. It hurts but the lie, the lack of respect and honoring of you as a person, is where the emotional and mental battle rages.

183

That very same night, after I had cried and screamed and thought and cried some more, at about 10 p.m., I got in my red sports car and drove three hours to my mom's home in Michigan. I climbed in the bed and stayed there. I believe I came back Monday morning. As far as I know, he was the first and only man that ever cheated on me, at least the only one who fessed-up or got caught. Unfortunately, in my early twenties, I really had no clue of genuine pure love beyond the physical, material and superficial. It took five months to work my way out of that relationship and not keep trying to hold on. Five months to work on my way of thinking, my way of living, my way of doing, my way of needing, my way of being.

It took a few years to be free of the soul ties of him and the others. It can take time for you to disconnect from your thoughts and memories, relearn you and truly learn to love and appreciate yourself. This is why having time between relationships is so important to your emotional, spiritual and mental health. I earnestly believe that when a relationship starts and continues wrong, out of order, in sin and lust, it cannot end right, unless both parties confess that wrong/sin and set things in order. That is when God will bless...bless it to continue or bless you by allowing it to end, so who He has for you can come. Unfortunately, trying to hold on to and continue with what God has not blessed or ordained is not beneficial. Even for some who have gone all the way to "I do" and are now facing challenges – ready to give up when the struggles come – just let it go.

We often try to hold on to what is not good or purposed for us because we are needy, don't want to be alone, don't know who we are or what we want. God is able to heal, reconcile and restore even what started wrong. He can turn it around and bless us through our

184

obedience to confess, repent and trust God. Seek to love, value and appreciate you first, and then expect the same from whoever God sends for you.

So you ask, "Have I loved again?" Yes, a couple of times. Did my love find me saying "I do – I will?" Yes. He was a Godly purposed man, four years my junior; yet, the most mature, wisest, caring guy I have ever met. He was as close to perfect as I thought I could get, but it did not work out. Simply put, wrong time/wrong place in our lives.

So today, with great joy and anticipation, with a full and happy life serving God, I wait patiently, expectantly on God – my Father to send me the man after His own heart to give me away to the true love of my life. Soon our paths will cross. A happy end of the matter it will be. You are the one and I (we) do not have to look for another. The best, the real, is yet to come.

Cheating in the Next Room

I was just fifteen when I met Tony. He had just recently gotten his first car, a two door Cutlass. He picked me up for a ride and we spent the afternoon, just kicking it. Tony asked me if I was a virgin. I was too humiliated to tell the truth. I told him no. I wanted to impress Tony, he was fine and he was on the boxing team. We ended up having sex that night, in his new Cutlass. Tony ended up going to jail later on that night. He was released the next day.

Immediately afterward our first sexual encounter, he started asking if I thought I was pregnant. He wanted me to get pregnant. We spent the next few weeks trying to make sure he got his wish. We had sex every day, several times a day and anywhere we could. I began to travel with the boxing team. We even had sex on the bus.

I developed a yeast infection and had to tell my mother. After going to the Doctor, we found out that I was in fact, pregnant. My mother hit the roof and immediately got Tony on the phone demanding his half of the money for the abortion. However, within fifteen minutes, she was on the phone, excited, telling someone that, we were going to have a baby.

For a brief moment, we were happy. His boxing career was promising. At a point soon after that, he developed the notion, that the baby was not his and became very distant. He lost interest in me and the baby, and began to concentrate on his two careers, boxing and pushing dope.

I was devastated and attempted suicide by taking some pills. After having my stomach pumped, I survived and the baby was fine.

Tony went to jail again. I started spending a lot of time with his family, (as my mom and I were always fussing; even to the point where she called Child Protective Services on me). I moved out and began trying to support myself by braiding hair while I attempted to finish school.

I eventually met a very nice man. He listened to me and was concerned about me, and my child. We soon moved in with him. He was safe. He was good. I should have been happy. But, I guess part of me craved the excitement of the drama in the streets.

I guess you sometimes find what you are looking for and I did not have to go far to find it. There was plenty of drama going on right in my own family. I found out that my own aunt, was having an affair with one of my old boyfriends. How dare she? I decided to retaliate against her and made plans to have an affair with one of her exes.

My plan did not go as planned. I intended to use him and move on just to spite her. I had a good man at home already. My plan failed. I actually fell in love with my aunt's ex-boyfriend. We really hit it off! He spoiled me with gifts, jewelry and money. Yes, I still lived with the "nice, go to work, take care of me, good man", but this "bad boy", I was cheating in the next room with, was a dream come true.

I had the best of both worlds. Mr. Right was so nice to me, but my heart was with Mr. Wrong. I could not stand to treat Mr. Right so deceitfully, so I plotted to move out of his apartment while he was at work. His brother, caught me loading my belongings into a cab, and pleaded his brother's case, "He's good to you---he loves you, don't do him like this."

He was right, when my own family was at odds with me, he was there for me. He provided a roof over our heads and he was a hard working man. He was respectful. He treated my child as his, not too much on the physical side, but he was Mr. Dependable.

I directed the cab to take me back to the apartment and I moved my stuff back in before he came home from work.

I often hear folks say "God don't like ugly." My little scheme soon all came crashing down at my feet. My aunt got wind of what I was doing and planned her pay back.

I remember one day arriving at my grandmother's house. There were some other people there with my aunt. Immediately the other lady began questioning me. "Is that my car you are driving?" "Wait, that is my necklace and my rings!" I knew trouble was at my doorstep. I texted my boyfriend and to my surprise he freaked out. Come to find out, the other lady was his estranged wife. He had been "recycling" by giving me her stuff!

I quickly called my stepdad. I needed to get out of this house. My grandmother and I had been on shaky terms. My aunt set all of this up and the other lady, well you can imagine her reaction. All the while, my boyfriend was texting me like crazy. "What is she doing now?" "What is going on, OMG!" It was a major circus in there and I felt like the number one clown.

When my stepfather arrived. I was so relieved. All of a sudden the other lady stopped all of her yelling and cussing. It was as though a light bulb went off in her head. She looked at my stepfather and said, "I know...you took my man, so I am going to take yours!" She looked at my stepfather and looked at me for my response. I quickly gathered my belongings and headed for the door. I looked back briefly. She was looking smug with an, "I got you now" look on her face, waiting for my response. Continuing out the door, I turned and gave her my response, "You got to deal with my momma on that one."

In the safety of my stepfather's car, I realized that sometimes-living life in the fast lane you can get more than you bargain for.

I was hurt realizing that my "man on the side" was cheating on me! He was still texting me, wanting to know what happened. We talked. He apologized and asked me what could he do to make it up to me. We settled for a thousand dollars and some new jewelry. I scolded him for cheating on me. He promised not to do it again.

I gathered my belongings, said thank you and goodbye to my stepfather and went into my apartment. I was thankful, I still had a few hours to calm my nerves, before my man got off work.

Unconditional Love

We were laughing and talking on the phone. I loved talking to Charles. I was fourteen. He was seventeen. I could not believe he was interested in me. I was the envy of all of the high school girls. Charles was one handsome man.

During our conversation, he asked me to hold the line for a moment. He heard some commotion. No one could have ever imagined the tragedy that would follow that moment.

I soon found out, that Charles's father had just been shot. When Charles arrived upstairs in their home, the only person there with his father, was his mother. His dad died in his arms.

There were weeks of detectives, court hearings and psychiatric evaluations etc. In the midst of all of this, I was trying to adjust to our new baby and being a newly wed. I was only 14.

Charles quickly grew abusive, drinking and using drugs. I attributed it all to the trauma that had gone on in his life. I was determined to stand by my man.

Years of more of the same…three children…trying to leave, but always coming back. No matter what he did, I would get angry and upset, but I felt that I was the only hope he had and I couldn't leave him when he was down. Year after year, I continued to stay.

In the beginning, when he messed up he would later be apologetic. As the years went by, no apologies, no sorry. This was just the way it was.

I eventually got a good job. I rationalized that perhaps some of the reason I stayed was financial. The other part was, as crazy as it sounds, I loved him, as he was the father of my children. But on the other hand, I most definitely was not in love with him. Sure, I had dreamed of the perfect marriage and perfect family life. But, despite my dreaming, wishing, and praying, Charles was headed at break neck speed down a road I did not want to travel.

I finally left and got a divorce. It is so strange. All of those years I thought I was staying to help Charles, I was really enabling him to continue down the same destructive path. My children who had grown up seeing all of the drama in our lives, had already grown tired of their father's lifestyle. On the other hand, I was yet trying to bail the water out of the sinking ship we called home.

When I finally left, the storm eventually calmed down. Charles got some help and eventually made a u-turn away from the destructive path he had followed all of these years. I cannot say that I stopped loving him, he was the father of my children, we had shared thirty-eight years of our lives together. But, I can say that for once, in thirty-eight years, with God's help, I finally realized that the first person I needed to love unconditionally was me.

"Power is the ability to walk away from something you desire . . . to protect something you love."

Author Unknown

Sistahwit

"The essence of who you are is often covered by all the defenses; insecurities, and adaptations that have accumulated over the years."

Robin Rice

"Take a ceremonial forgiveness shower/bath. Using a favorite soap/body wash, with yourself in your own compassion, imagining the deadness of unresolved pain and guilt going down the drain. Thank the pain and guilt for serving its purpose. Which was to let you know your own true values. Step forth whole, authentic, and free to make new choices with the True You as a guide."

Robin Rice

" The roles have reversed. We as women have empowered men to believe they are our gods. Therefore, we are sometimes chasing men who mean us no good and losing our self-worth in the process. Every now and then individuals will leave us by walking out of our lives. It is amazing the lengths we will go to get them back. Including but not limited to making complete fools of our selves. In some cases, it is the will of God that the individual left in order for God to do a work in us."

LaJoy M. Tyree

"You can't depend on your eyes when your imagination is out of focus."

Mark Twain

"For it was not into my ear you whispered, but into my heart, it was not my lips you kissed, but my soul."

Judy Garland

"The way a man treats his mother is an absolute prerequisite for continuing any type of relationship. If he does not respect and treat his mother right, then there is no need to even speak the next word."

Princess Harris

"But who can distinguish between falling in love and imagining falling in love? Even genuinely falling in love is an act of the imagination."

Author Unknown

"When I eventually met Mr. Right I had no idea that his first name was Always."

Rita Rudner

Everything in your life, every experience, every relationship is a mirror of the mental pattern that's going on inside of you.   Louise L. Hay

"Life is too short to fake anything."

Author Unknown

JUST FOR FUN!

The Mr. Right/Wrong

Basic Questionnaire

The Basics

1. Name

2. Address

3. Home Phone

4. Work Number

5. Cell Phone (All of them)

6. Email Address

7. Facebook Name

The Required

8. Age

9. Height

10. Weight

11. Who are you living with? (i.e., Mother, Father, Grandmother, baby's Momma, Homeboy, sister, etc.)

12 Do you have a valid driver's license?

13. Do you own a car? Include make, model year and is it running? Are your car payments up to date?

14. Diseases. Have you ever had any of the following:

Hepatitis A B or C

Mononucleosis

HIV/AIDS

Crabs

West Niles Virus

Chlamydia

Gonorrhea

SARS

Head Lice

Ringworms

Sex Change

Herpes

Any Mental Illness

15. Are you addicted to:

Crack/Cocaine

Heroin

Paint/Markers

Ecstasy

Glue

Pills

Snuff

16. Have you ever been incarcerated? If so, state the following:

Date   Crime   Time Served

17. Are you in a relationship now?

18. Have you ever been married?

19. How many children do you have?

20. How many children do you suspect may be yours?

21. How many children are you in denial of?

22. How many different "Baby Mommas" do you have?

23. Are you or any of your "Baby Mommas" crazy?

24. Have any of your "Baby Mommas" served time?

Please attach a copy of the following:

[ ] Most recent pay stub

[ ] Social Security Card

[ ] A recent Doctor's statement indicating a clean bill of health

[ ] Any and all divorce papers

[ ] List three (3) personal references

Words to Ponder...

Emotion: A strong surge of feeling marked by an impulse of outward expression and often accompanied by complex bodily reactions; any strong feeling, as love hate or joy.

Right: Conformable to the truth or fact; correct.

Wrong: not correct, mistaken; erroneous; not suitable, inappropriate, improper.

Imagination: The mental ability to create original and striking images and concepts by recombining the products of past experience.

Chapter 7

The Seventh Man

*T*he Seventh Man

Jesus said to her, "Go, call your husband, and come back."
The woman answered him, "I have no husband." Jesus said
to her, "You are right in saying, "I have no husband"; for
you have had five husbands, and the one you have now is
not your husband. What you have said is true!"

John 4:16–18

After reading this book, I am in hopes that you have experienced some form of freedom. "He/she that the Son sets free is free indeed."

I would like to share the story listed below that I have titled "The Seventh Man". Sometime ago, I spoke at a Church and compared myself to the woman at the well (John 4:3-30) and let the audience know how I felt until I found the seventh man (Jesus), who I felt had freed my soul for all the issues I had experienced. Thank God, I survived my "Well Experience". The man who showed up in my life who knew everything, all my secrets, everything I did behind closed doors, in the dark that I felt would never show up in the light; the man who showed up in my life, although I felt I would never be able to fill the void nor find love again.

Jesus used water as a metaphor to teach this woman. He spoke about the living water, which gives eternal life, divine grace, or in other words, God's life within the soul. He made her to understand that she needed to confess her sins and change her life before she could obtain this life giving water — grace. Jesus showed her that He already knew she was living with a man who was not her husband. In my opinion, Jesus did not judge her, he wanted her to feel safe with him knowing that He knew who she really was and all the things she had done. She felt she could remove the various masks we wear as women each day. She was able to be real with this man.

While I was seated in the beauty shop a while ago, I asked the question, "What is it that can cause a woman to have five husbands and to later live with someone's husband? I wish you could have been there to hear how bad the women talked about who ever they thought it was. It amazed me how even today, several women are still trapped like the Samaritan woman was, obviously thirsty for love from a natural man. The affection of a man never seemed to satisfy her. She continued to look for love in all the wrong places. The Samaritan woman at the well was no angel. Mixed up with a wrong crowd, this poor woman from Samaria had quite a reputation. She probably hoped that the next man just might be the hero she was looking for. Jesus knew her thirst for love, just as he knows ours. I learned one lesson from the way the women talked so boldly about this woman: Confession is good for the soul, but bad for the reputation. Thank God, forgiveness is part of the benefit package of salvation!

Through her story, there is a lesson: people should not live by carnal pleasure. The story also shows that a well of grace is ready to refresh the soul parched by sin and suffering; and that Jesus comes to save the sick and to serve those who still need both physical and spiritual healing, not only the converted.

No one bothered to ask the woman about her hopes as she carried her one hope with her to the well. It was her last hope. She had to go to the well. She did not know it yet, but it was this, her last hope that would change her life. She found the seventh man. Jesus was at the well. He gave her what every woman wants in life, to belong, to be accepted and to be valued. Just like women of today, she was ashamed of who she really was, due to her style of living. Ashamed of herself because she had more than likely sold her soul just trying to make it through the night.

Hold on to your hope! Faith requires us to hold on to our hopes, not our fears. Everyone has fears but they have different names: loneliness, abandonment, low self-esteem, addictions, emptiness, health issues, grief, identity crises, unhealthy habits, unhealthy relationships, or pain. I encourage you to hold on to your last hope!

Many women have been wounded by poor decisions; decisions they made and decisions others made for them. If all you have left are broken pieces, gather them up and hold on to them until your dreams come true. Strengthen that which remains.

The other day my granddaughter De'Ja said to me, "Big dreams will happen." It is time to step to the well, meet the seventh man and enter into a new season of power. Let the weak say I'm strong. As women, we must be careful to guard our hearts. There is a song that says, "Every time you go away, you take a piece of me with you." That should not be! If Ray Ray leaves you, you should keep your pieces so you don't end up having to go across town and or across the country collecting the pieces back. The collection process is sometimes the hardest piece to the puzzle. Hold on to yourself first, prior to trying to hold on to someone else.

Maybe you have a past that you have brought into your present situation and you see no way out. Maybe you have a problem like I had, of not being able to forgive myself for the misdeeds I had done. If so, it is my prayer that not just for today, but from this point on that you will start your new life of being restored, and that you will arrive at the appointed time with nothing missing and nothing broken!

Be Liberated

Pamelia Tyree-Carr

*S*oul Ties Prayer

(Author Unknown)

Father God:

Thank you for saving me from destruction. I praise you for sending Jesus to die for my sins. Specifically, I confess that I have sinned in the following ways: _____ (details of the sin & names).

I repent from those sins and renounce them now. Please forgive me and cleanse my conscience with the blood of Jesus. Lord, please cut the unhealthy soul ties between me and _____ (list name (s)).

Please restore me to wholeness in spirit, soul and body and reintegrate any part of me that was involved with those soul ties. I also ask for the salvation and restoration of those people that I was involved with. I commit him/her/them to your care. I rebuke any evil spirits that may have gained a foothold in me from that sin and I command them to leave me and go to Jesus Christ now!

Thank you, Lord, for setting me free to live as the new person in Christ you made me to be! I praise you now and forever,

Amen

To Contact

Pamelia Tyree-Carr

For speaking engagements, book signings and events:

Email:

Womenofdestiny2001@yahoo.com

On Facebook: Pamelia Tyree-Carr

Mail:

Parablist Publishing House

P.O. Box 43379

Richmond Heights, OH 44143

www.parablistpublishinghouse.com

Group Discussion Questions

1. Give an example of a time you were willing to put yourself in harm's way for what initially appeared to be love and happiness. Refer to the story regarding Rufus in this book.

2. What is your definition of a "soul tie"?

3. Is the quote written by Alan D. Washington that says, " "Once the door of abuse opens, it never closes" true? If so, give an example of the warning signs of an abusive relationship you or a close friend or relative has experienced.

4. How can you tell if a man has signs of being a "Down Low Brother" or living a double life? "Gay/Straight" or just "Gay", would you date a man of this nature? Do you feel there are health risks involved?

5. Give an example of a relationship where you thought you had landed Mr. Right but he turned out to be Mr. Wrong.

6. Do you feel it is wrong to date a married man and/or a committed man? What does the Bible say about married couples?

7. What are the telltale signs of an uncommitted man?

8. Give an example of a time when you did not pay attention to the red flags and/or warning signs before entering what you thought was a sound relationship. What did it cost you?

Published By:

Parablist Publishing House

P.O. Box 43379

Richmond Heights, OH 44143

Email: parablistpublishing@yahoo.com

Additional copies can be purchased at:

www.parablistpublishinghouse.com

www.ingramcontent.com/pod-product-compliance
Lightning Source LLC
Chambersburg PA
CBHW071951090426
42740CB00011B/1893